PRAISE FOR WEBINARS, C

WITH JACK ELIAS

"I LOVE this webinar so very much. I have to mute sometimes because I am laughing so much at your surprising insights."
—**Steven F., Vermont, USA**

"Fantastic wisdom bombs, as always! Lots packed into your classes. Too good!"
—**Robbie M., Tokyo, Japan**

"I would have paid $10,000 for what I got from you in just one 90-minute session!"
—**David R., Corporate Executive**

"Just finished listening to the recording of your class for the second time. So beautiful and real. At times I was smiling, nodding, and weeping. Thank you for your amazing work and all it means to so many."
—**Ruth L., Washington, USA**

"Jack's work is full of heart. With his outstanding clarity, he has helped me correct fundamental flaws in my thinking process, resulting in an increase in overall energy and awareness. His effect on many patients I know has empowered them to change limiting beliefs that had handicapped them in their growth and expression."
—**Daniel Lewis, DC, Chiropractor**

"I have made important and necessary changes in my life as a result of your course—in my relationships, diet, daily schedule, therapeutic skill, and self-esteem. I feel like I'm coming alive to my life in a way not experienced before."
—**Adrian B., Addictions Counselor**

"I have learned more about love in this course than in the rest of my life."
—**Carol W., Home Care**

PRAISE FOR BOOKS AND TRAININGS BY CECI MILLER

"Ceci Miller writes with startling honesty, directness, and passion, but more than this: She accepts the challenge that Dante accepted seven centuries ago. She tries to express the inexpressible, so that others may benefit. There is no higher calling for a writer."

—**Tracy Daugherty**, author of *Hiding Man, Just One Catch*, and *The Last Love Song*

"A profound story of beauty and wisdom unfolding from within as the heart opens up. The insights and practices given here are exquisite blossoms."

—**Jamal Rahman**, author of *The Fragrance of Faith: The Enlightened Heart of Islam*

"Prepare to be touched by the wonders of grace."

—**Marci Shimoff,** author of *Chicken Soup for the Woman's Soul*

"Ceci Miller's frank advice on spiritual inquiry is a treasure not to be missed."

—**John Bradshaw**, author of *Healing the Shame that Binds You*

"Many of the exercises, ideas, and rich prose [in Writing from the Body] are Ceci's, and I'm happy to say I trust you've had a finer reading experience, thanks to her part in the book."

—**John Lee**, author of *The Flying Boy* and *Writing from the Body*

The Outrageous Guide
to Being Fully Alive

....

Defeat Your Inner Trolls
and Reclaim Your Sense of Humor

THE OUTRAGEOUS GUIDE TO BEING FULLY ALIVE

DEFEAT YOUR INNER TROLLS AND RECLAIM YOUR SENSE OF HUMOR

Jack Elias, CHT
and Ceci Miller, MFA

Published by Five Wisdoms Press
Seattle, Washington.

Cover design by Carlos Ferreyros.
Interior book design by Mi Ae Lipe, whatnowdesign.com.

For information about attending workshops and trainings,
or to book a private session or speaking engagement with Jack Elias,
visit JackElias.com.

For information about working with Ceci Miller, visit CeciBooks.com.
Learn about the Emotional Rescue Method and courses at
EmotionalRescue.info.

First Edition, 2021
ISBN: 978-0-9655210-3-1
Library of Congress Control Number: 2021900968

Contents

....

Acknowledgments   ix

Introduction   xi

1. Dealing with Expectations, Anxiety, and Stress   1

How to Deal with High Expectations   3

How to Deal with the Stress of a Big Project   7

The Best Way to Start and End Your Day Free of Stress and Anxiety   12

My Top 5 Tips for Dealing with Anxiety   16

How Not to Double Down on Your Anxiety   20

2. Anger, Hurt, Loneliness, Shyness, and Feeling like a Failure   25

How to Throw Away Hurt Feelings So They Don't Come Back   27

Why It's Important to Keep Your Sense of Humor   30

How to Enjoy Letting Go of Anger
and Other Inner Trolls in 4 Simple Steps   35

Overcoming Loneliness and Shyness: 7 Messages of Self-Respect   39

Feeling Like a Failure: The Oldest Con There Is   44

3. Befriending Yourself and Other Things Couples Need to Know   49

How to Be a Good Friend to Yourself   51

Why Mindfulness in Relationships Helps
You Make Better Choices   55

How to Stop Worrying in Relationships   59

The 3 Skills You Need If You Want to Help Others   61

3 Things All Couples Need to Know
to Improve Communication in Relationships   65

4. Mindfulness, Meditation, and Real Happiness 69

8 Ways to Develop Mindfulness and Awareness,
Plus One Imagination Game 71

10 Wrong Ideas That Can Ruin Your Mindfulness Practice 76

You Can Meditate 82

Simple Meditation Instructions 85

What If I Don't Have Time for Meditation? 87

Is Your Problem Time Management or FOMO? 91

5. Worry and Self-Doubt, Kindness and Confidence 97

Feeling Helpless? 99

How to Stop Worrying and Enjoy Making Plans 102

How to Invite Success 106

How Can I Be More Kind? 110

5 Ways to Transform Fear and Self-Doubt
into Peace and Happiness 115

How Can I Be More Confident? 118

6. Facing Illness, Aging, Death, and the Holidays 121

Dealing with a Diagnosis of Terminal Illness 123

How to Deal with the Fear of Aging and Death 129

How Bad Holiday Memories Can Actually Help You 133

Getting Clear about Fear 136

How to Keep Your Courage in the Age of the
Pandemic, Terrorism, and Climate Change 141

About the Authors 143

Acknowledgments

....

I AM GRATEFUL TO my clients and students. Their courage and tenderheartedness inspire me every day to refresh my understanding of the powerfully transformative instructions I have received from my teachers. Keeping my relationship to these instructions fresh enables me to constantly improve the help and support I offer to others in my counseling practice and courses.

I am thankful for my children Sarah, Karen, John, and Andrew Elias. They opened my heart from the moment they were born and thereafter, on a daily basis, have given me precious opportunities to practice being kind, loving, and patient and to forgive myself when I was not.

My wife, Ceci Miller, with great love and patience, has always seen and encouraged the best in me. With her skill as a writer and as the principal editor of all my work, she has made it possible to communicate the insights in these pages with vastly greater clarity than I ever could have done on my own.

Everything I have to offer that is beneficial comes from studying and practicing with precious spiritual teachers: Shunryū Suzuki Roshi, Chögyam Trungpa Rinpoche, His Holiness the 16th Karmapa Rangjung Rigpe Dorje, Khenpo Tsültrim Gyamtso Rinpoche, Baba Muktananda, Gurumayi Chidvilasananda, and Dzogchen Ponlop Rinpoche. I can never repay their great kindness, which is a constant blessing to myself, my family, and all of my clients and students. My teachers are the cause of all of the benefit you will find here.

—Jack Elias

Thank you to all of my clients and workshop participants these many years for your openness in sharing your struggles and in meeting your hardships with courage and kindness.

To my dear friends, especially Carlos Ferreyros, Dr. Diane Gregorio, and Cindy Shelton, thank you for your constant loving support in so many forms, seen and unseen.

To my family, deep gratitude for lessons that can be learned nowhere else! I love you all beyond words.

Thank you with all my heart to Dzogchen Ponlop Rinpoche, Khenpo Tsültrim Gyamtso Rinpoche, and to all the mahasiddhas for giving the key instructions that open the door to wisdom. With love, songs, and laughter, you light the way to the intrinsic health and wisdom that is the birthright of every being.

Readers, thank you for your interest and attention. Wherever in this book you encounter clear awareness and awakening wisdom, it is solely due to our kind teachers. For any errors you find, we are responsible.

—Ceci Miller

Introduction

....

HOWEVER YOU DISCOVERED THIS book, I'm glad you did. It is a sign of wisdom to seek insight into a persistent struggle in a relationship, at work, with our parents or children, or with a general sense of uncertainty about our place and purpose in the world.

Gathered in this small collection are favorite, go-to approaches to the problems my clients have most often presented over the years. For ease in the reading, this book is written in first person. The content offered here, however, is the product of a fruitful 20-year collaboration with my wife and coauthor, Ceci Miller.

In my workshops, webinars, and private sessions; in the Finding True Magic course in Transpersonal Hypnosis and Hypnotherapy/NLP based on my book of the same name; and in Ceci's long experience writing books on human development as well as coaching authors and leading trainings, we have both marveled at the common ground we all travel in our search to make this precious human life meaningful.

For 4 decades, Ceci and I have each had the good fortune to work with many people who were kind enough to share with us the rapid, positive results they experienced by applying the very insights and exercises you will find throughout this book.

The exercises here are arranged by theme to make it easy to find what most directly applies to the specific challenge you are facing at any given time. We hope this book will be a good friend to you on your journey, and that by using it, you will become an even better friend to yourself.

May you enjoy the explorations offered here. As you apply these methods, may you discover the awakening wisdom and miraculous healing capacity of your own good heart.

1

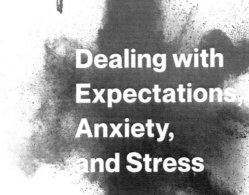

Dealing with Expectations, Anxiety, and Stress

How to Deal
with
High Expectations

....

WHEN WE TALK ABOUT HOW to deal with "high expectations," what do we mean? Whether we're worried about other people's high expectations of us, or we're besieged by our own high expectations of ourselves, we need to know just what we mean when we use this phrase.

Having worked with clients and students for many years, I've noticed that we are often extremely skilled at deluding and torturing ourselves. How do we do it? We speak using virtuous-sounding euphemisms for what are actually harsh and fear-inducing judgments. In my opinion, that is the case with the phrase "high expectations."

The notion of high expectations seems to sync up nicely with the idea of "doing your best" or "being all you can be." Who would argue with such apparently noble ideas? Isn't it a good thing to expect the best of yourself, or for others to expect the best of you? Maybe. But let's take a closer look at that idea.

If you've ever felt stressed out and anxious at work, you've probably experienced the tyranny of high expectations. When someone is always looking over your shoulder to see if you're going to succeed at accomplishing their high expectations, this noble label doesn't encourage or inspire you. We don't feel at ease, or spacious, or joyfully engaged in our efforts.

So, why do we buy into the idea of other people's high expectations for us? Because we don't allow ourselves to question this idea or walk away from it. We construct this self-imposed prison…built on a general fear and lack of clarity about our life.

This issue of high expectations comes into play at home, at work, or at school—with family and friends, with coworkers, associates, and teachers.

It's not much of a problem in any of our relationships with others—as long as we have real clarity about 3 key aspects of our life. Gaining clarity about them makes all the difference in our world.

GAINING CLARITY ABOUT EXPECTATIONS: 3 KEY INSIGHTS

1. **Confusion about ownership.** Family and bosses often have a subtle or not-so-subtle attitude of owning you, their employee, or child. But in order to live an authentic life, it is crucial to recognize that no one owns you. When you are authentically yourself, you easily recognize and honor what you genuinely like and dislike. Then it's easy to say yes to what you genuinely want to say yes to, and to say no to what you want to say no to. But if you're caught in the game of being owned by others, you're like a planet orbiting around someone else's sun. This happens when the strong habitual posture of dependency that we develop in childhood intrudes on what should be our experience of authentic adulthood.

    If we and our parents haven't worked together to "cut the apron strings," we enter adulthood still in the psychological posture of a dependent child. We act out behavior patterns that we should have outgrown. When we operate under the impression that our life is not our own, then a parent, boss, or anyone else who doesn't honor our autonomy can easily take advantage of our immature state.

    To gain clarity about owning your own life, first discover your genuine values and interests. Then begin to honor those values and interests by honestly expressing your authentic yeses and your authentic nos.

2. **Confusion about adulthood.** Whether it's a family member's disapproval or the prospect of a boss firing you, fear of rejection presents a powerful obstacle for many of us. But this fear gains power only when we lack clarity about our adulthood. Without this clarity, we're easily pulled away from our true values and aims. So, how do we live an authentic life? We practice staying present in genuine adult consciousness.

   Of course, human "adulthood" is defined differently in an economic context than it is in that of our psychological health. But here we are referring to adulthood as an internal framework through which we navigate our world relatively independently, with a basic sense of courage and confidence.

   So, how do we know if we're confused about our adulthood? We need look no further than the fear of rejection.

   The only person for whom rejection is a real existential problem is a child.

   A child is not equipped to care for and support herself. Thus, our definition of "adult" here is one who is self-supporting and self-validating. When we go into fear of rejection or into any fearful state, we are regressing into the psychological state of a frightened child who knows they can't handle this experience. The child expects to be told what to do and hopes to be rescued. An adult, however, meets the world with courage and self-respect. No matter what happens, the adult does not abandon or compromise their true values and aims.

   Can you see how, if you accept being owned by others and thus are afraid of their rejection, the phrase "high expectations" becomes a tenacious trap? The threatened child believes that only if they perform "well"—by living up to the high expectations of their "owners"—can they survive!

3. **Confusion about performance.** Let's assume that you have freed yourself from a sense of other-ownership and from the

fear of rejection by others. That's great! However, you still may lack clarity about how you work, what makes you tick, and how best to engage the world. You may not know what it means to you to perform at your best. And, in the absence of judgment by others, what does "your best" mean?

When you are living as an authentic adult, you know what your genuine interests are. Then doing your best means engaging in those activities with whole-hearted joyful focus. You are genuinely interested in your activities. You focus on them because you made a genuine choice to serve your true aim by means of this activity—not to please or avoid displeasing someone else. As an authentic adult, you understand that life is a learning curve and mistakes are gifts, not stigmas.

Mistakes show you where you lack knowledge. Mistakes also alert you to when you've lost focus and attention. Such wakeup calls can be dramatic and even painful, but they are never biased; they are not nasty, judgmental punishment. Mistakes are simply the law of cause and effect giving you feedback about how you have fallen off the learning curve. As an adult, you simply learn the lesson and begin again— this time a bit more intelligently. You keep a sense of joyful self-encouragement. Mistakes are how we learn! The law of cause and effect is always at our side to guide us and wake us up.

As you unpack these insights, you will easily leave behind worrying about fulfilling the high expectations of others (living in fear and confusion). You will discover and feel life creating you and meeting you and guiding you, inwardly and outwardly, moment by moment, day by day, in every way.

It is life that does that! Not your parents and not anybody else. You are completely free to enjoy getting to know life, your true support, while becoming your own best friend.

How to Deal
with the Stress
of a Big Project

....

SOMEONE RECENTLY ASKED ME, "When you're working on a big project, how do you deal with the stress?!"

Throughout Western society, we seem to hold the attitude that, if something is important, we must generate a fearful, stressed-out state of mind about accomplishing it.

How does this stress get started? By expecting ourselves to produce nothing less than the highest performance and perfect outcomes. These expectations produce only stress for everyone involved and rarely result in favorable outcomes—in business, at home, or in school—or anywhere else in our lives.

In my study and training in Zen Buddhist discipline, I encountered a wonderful bit of wisdom that is relevant to our habit of adding stress as soon as we take on a big project:

"How you do one thing is how you do everything."

Of course, regarding the superficial aspect of our efforts, this statement doesn't apply. Every step in a project requires a different kind of activity. We don't do everything at the same speed. And we don't do everything with the same level of physical exertion. That would be silly and impractical.

So, this Zen teaching statement is not a one-liner manual of project management!

This wisdom teaching goes much deeper than that. It points toward our deepest attitudes about life. It asks us to look at the very nature of taking action and achieving outcomes.

Throughout our lives, we're constantly working with relationships—the relationship to ourselves, to one another and, even when we're alone, to our environment.

In my view, this Zen statement is, first and foremost, urging us to look deeply at how we relate to our life, our body, and our mind.

Are we taking our healthy body, our intelligent mind, and our relatively abundant outer resources for granted? Do we find it easy to complain and are we quick to judge? These behaviors may indicate a sense of entitlement that colors all of our thinking. We may be lacking an important sense of mystery and gratitude about our life and circumstances.

If this is the case, we are easily susceptible to being hard on ourselves, hard on others, and hard on our environment (don't throw that spoon!) whenever things aren't going our way.

Are we ruled by the belief that we SHOULD get what we want—just because we want it?

This is the natural attitude of young children. Little ones do not yet understand the laws of cause and effect, so we help them learn: "If you run downhill and fall, you can get hurt." "If you don't share the toy with your new friend, she may not want to play with you."

From childhood to adulthood, we must learn that the laws of cause and effect must be accurately followed to get the outcomes we want. You can't plant lemon seeds and get apples for your trouble, no matter how much you may want that to happen!

If you have a big, important project to accomplish, your assessment of its importance does not affect these laws of cause and effect in the least. You must always act in accordance with those laws if you are to get the best results.

3 CRUCIAL THINGS TO APPRECIATE
ABOUT THE LAWS OF CAUSE AND EFFECT

1. Recognize that the laws of cause and effect govern ALL activities: mental, emotional, physical, and environmental.

2. All activity is most powerful and functional when all of the energies involved—mental, emotional, and physical—are flowing freely, without restraint.

3. What is restraint? Fearful thinking is restraint. Anger, jealousy, and greed are restraint. Worry and blame are restraint. Compulsiveness, distraction (or inability to focus), and anxious speediness are restraint.

All activities of restraint share the same basic flaw: They are all activities by which we squeeze ourselves mentally, emotionally, and physically. And when we squeeze ourselves, we also squeeze and harm our environment. How we do one thing is how we do everything.

HOW AND WHY TO AVOID SQUEEZING YOURSELF

1. **First: Relax!** Bring your attention to your body and breath as often as you can. Breathe with gratitude for the gift of life, the breath that you are receiving right now. Encourage your busy mind to enjoy taking in this gift of breath, fully and with ease.

2. **Appreciate the temporary nature of your life.** This helps to reset your inner attitude so that you can stay loose and good-natured. Remember that your ability to exert yourself is a gift and a wonder. Start today to master the ability to relax into every kind of activity you engage in. How you do one thing is how you do everything.

3. **Remember that nothing is required.** Everything is chosen. Own your choices. And remember that you are at your best when you stay in the flow of your energies, free of squeezing.

4. **You will easily stay inspired to release squeezing when you remember that squeezing is its own stand-alone activity.** Squeezing yourself never contributes energy or clarity to your efforts. It is always a drain and disruptor of your flow.

When you make these simple, verifiable insights your guiding principles, you will develop the ability to stay mentally and emotionally cheerful, creative, and kind. You will be able to maintain this cheerful, kind attitude even if your projects are not accomplished exactly as you had hoped.

Projects that fail to meet expectations don't mean you're a failure. They are not a demand or requirement that you take negative actions mentally, emotionally, or physically. Such outcomes are simply giving you the gift of feedback. They let you know that you need to learn more about how to relate to the laws of cause and effect in order to accomplish your expectations.

IN A NUTSHELL—MY VERSION OF THIS ZEN APHORISM
Who knows if wonderful wisdom is accurately quoted? Who says it can't be modified to be more easily understood?

Considering this Zen aphorism, I understand it more clearly when I read it as,

"How you do THE ONE THING is how you do everything."

How I do the one inner thing determines how I relate to everything else. What is "the one thing"? It is our attitude toward ourselves—our relationship to the one we are with all the time.

If I take my life for granted and disregard my value as a human being and my feelings, this is how I will treat everyone and everything else, too.

If I make sure that "the one thing" is to practice loving, encouraging self-regard—and if I do this with gratitude and wonder for the gift of life moment by moment—that attitude will infuse everything I do with uplifting energy.

Everything we do flows from and is colored by our inner state of self-relationship. May you find it easier and easier to do The One (loving) Thing.

The Best Way to Start
and End Your Day
Free of Stress and Anxiety

....

Do you start and end your day immediately thinking about your "To Do" list or your "To Avoid" list or a mix of both?

If so, you may have gotten used to a constant level of stress and anxiety and a speedy thinking mind that jumps from one line of thought to another: "I absolutely have to finish that report today" ... "I have to get these lunches ready in 15 minutes before we head out the door" ... "Where did I put the good spreading knife?" ... "I probably won't get home in time to eat dinner with the kids ..."

We usually believe that stress and anxiety is caused by our To Do lists and the demands on our time. But if we think our circumstances are the cause of our stress, we inevitably think of ourselves as victims. In that frame of mind, stress and anxiety will seem to be reasonable reactions—because it's quite true that we're not in control of certain circumstances.

But what would happen to our stress and anxiety level if we could change the way we think about circumstances and our To Do lists? What if we recognized that we are in control of feeling out of control? What if we could slow down our frantic minds?

Initially we may think, "It can't be done" or "Not much would change!" We will be stuck if we have a "Yeah, but ..." response to these ideas. We may accept them, then object to them, and then notice that we don't feel different right away if we try acting on them. In that case, we risk dismissing the whole idea without really making a substantial effort. And then? We're highly likely to jump right back into our habit of speedy, anxious thinking.

The most important insight here is, "I am in control of feeling out of control right now." But even this crucial insight won't matter unless we go beyond just considering it.

We must make a commitment to effectively act on it.

So, how do we get beyond "Good idea, but…" and make this shift from a stressed-out, ineffective speedy reaction to calm, effective action?

2 HYPNOSIS TIPS TO HELP YOU GET INSPIRED AND STAY INSPIRED

Two powerful, innate capacities are on our side, empowering us to make the shift from speedy stress to ease if we engage them: the hypnotic power of our mind and the habit-forming power of our mind.

So, the first tip: Notice hypnotic moments—waking up and falling asleep. "Hypnotic" simply means "open to suggestion and change." And typically, every day we completely overlook 2 naturally occurring hypnotic moments of opportunity.

Practice noticing these hypnotic moments and use them to install powerful positive suggestions in your mind: One is the **hypnopompic state**, which arises immediately before your thinking mind wakes up, and the **hypnagogic state**, which arises immediately after your thinking mind falls asleep.

In both of these hypnotic moments, the same amazing thing happens. Upon waking in the morning, before the speedy thinking mind grabs all your attention, you will be in the hypnopompic state. This is a moment of quiet calm awareness, in which you can experience a taste of the sweetness of simply being alive.

In a similar way, as you are just starting to fall asleep, if you make the effort to stay awake and watch the moment when the thinking mind begins to fall away, you will be in the hypnogogic state. Once again, you will be able to experience the same calm sweetness of being alive.

So, how does this help you transform your stress into peaceful ease?

When you catch each of these hypnotic moments, you are going to be highly receptive to suggestions and positive change. These are moments of potential transformation.

Here's a good classic hypnotic suggestion: "I am getting better and better every day in every way."

Just easily repeat this or any positive suggestion, over and over, 21 times.

You can do this first thing in the morning when you're in the hypnopompic state, or as you are falling asleep at night while you're in the hypnogogic state.

You don't have to worry about catching these hypnotic moments perfectly. Just practice noticing the first moment of waking and the last moment of wakefulness before you go to sleep, and then repeat a positive affirmation during these times.

Now for my second tip: Use hypnotic repetition—the habit-forming power. It is encouraging to remember that we have a built-in habit-forming capacity. If we act repeatedly in a positive way, we will develop a positive habit... guaranteed! After only a short time—27 days or less—your new positive action will become effortless, especially if you practice in the general atmosphere of the hypnopompic and hypnagogic states.

Practicing with these 2 tips can free yourself from discouraging thoughts about "how hard it is to change." That kind of thinking just stops us from repeating the positive action enough times to make it an effortless positive habit.

So, for the next week, just try making the easy effort to notice these 2 moments of awareness:

- just before the thinking mind arises as you wake up, and

- just after the thinking mind drops away as you're going to sleep.

At first, don't even worry about repeating the positive suggestion. Just enjoy the sweet moment of awareness before and after the thinking mind grabs your attention.

Resting in this awareness is the very source of empowerment for your positive suggestions.

Remember: You create and guarantee positive results with repeated practice. So, keep it going!

My Top 5 Tips
for Dealing with Anxiety

ANXIETY—WHAT IS IT GOOD FOR? Absolutely nothin'! I am speaking to myself as much as to you today, because over the years I've noticed there's a sneaky quality to my anxiety. Now, whenever I notice it creeping up, I have certain ways of talking to myself to rouse the courage to *challenge* this self-defeating attitude. Here are my top 5 tips for dealing with anxiety and fear of failure:

1. **Anxiety is a luxury.**
   Anxiety is not necessarily a material luxury, because obviously you can be poor and anxious. You may not realize it, but we have to have an attitude of luxury about our time even to be able to "do anxiety." I have to feel I can afford to spend time on my hobby of anxious thinking. Because let's face it: Anxious thinking and worry take up time and energy.

   Somewhere deep down, I must have decided that my most heartfelt goals can wait. How do I know this? Because I always seem to have the luxury of wasting my intelligence and energy—anxiously worrying, spinning inside a "poor me" hamster wheel. I'm just spinning away, spending time. But is it a luxury I can afford?

2. **Anxiety + fear-of-failure fantasies = procrastination.**
   It starts like this: I'm about to begin to address some issue—a project, a goal, a resolution. But then I have a thought: "What's going to happen if I start focusing my energy in some

productive way to meet this challenge?" I might fail in never-before-dreamed-of ways! Onto the wheel I hop, and the spinning begins. And my heartfelt goal? Oh, it can wait. Anxiety often masquerades as procrastination. We avoid taking action on our goals and choose instead to obsess in anxious thinking—because it delays the possibility of making a mistake. We meet up with a fear of failure, and then we freeze. Instead of taking action, we make a withdrawal from our luxurious bank account of extra time and energy, and we spend it putting off making our best effort. We think we're avoiding failure, but...

3. **What's failure got to do with it? Absolutely nothin'!**
    Have you ever been in a fight? If so, you know that whatever anxiety you had about the fight disappears once you're actually engaged in the act of fighting. If you're attacked, fighting back is an appropriate course of ACTION, and you plan and make course corrections moment by moment. You act and make adjustments according to the results you get. You don't freeze and obsessively think, "What if I do this...what if I do that...what if...oh, my God!" (If you stop to do that, you'll get clobbered!)

4. **When you're anxious—ACT NOW.**
    The main remedy for my anxiety is to start taking action...now! Of course, I can only take action now (when else would I do it?). But I have to remind myself of now, because I so easily fantasize taking action in the future. "I'll do it as soon as..." The problem is, the future never becomes now and now is the only time I can act!

    You can't be anxious **now** if you're focused on this moment—you can only act and make course corrections in the subsequent moments of **now** as they arise. You can only be anxious if you're focused on the past and the future, bouncing back and forth, fearfully concerned about "poor me."

5. **Don't try. Just do. (Thanks, Yoda and Nike.)**
In my transpersonal hypnotherapy trainings, one of the first points we cover is how to talk to your subconscious mind to get that mind to ACT in your best interests:

"The hypnotic suggestion is always stated in the present tense. You must recognize that the 'subconscious' mind lives in the now. The mind that is able to cause change lives in the now, and changes things in the now. Everything is happening now; therefore you do things now, you don't 'try' to do things." (That's a direct quote from my book, Finding True Magic, page 16.)

"Trying" to do things is delaying doing things. And delaying means putting things off to the future. It means I'm acting as if I have the luxury of spending time as if I have forever. And as we NOW know … the future never comes!

What happens if I forget my own top 5 tips? I don't beat myself up. I just keep ACTING. I practice making my best choice and my best effort now, moment by moment. You and I have what it takes to turn our minds in a positive direction. We can meet any challenge that has caught our attention, unconcerned with how we may be judged by others—success or failure, fool or hero—it doesn't matter. I'm the one who decides to stop spinning. I choose to move forward. Fear is a luxury I can't afford, and **anxiety, what is it good for? Absolutely nothing!**

Good luck!

If you'd like to go further in accomplishing your heartfelt goals, check out *Developing True Heart Intuition and Self-Integration*. This experiential seminar is 1 of 5 in my Living from the

Heart Collection, and it's brimming with techniques I've often been told are life-changing for those who apply them. You'll find it and other valuable programs in the Finding True Magic online shop at shop.findingtruemagic.com.

How Not
to Double Down
on Your Anxiety

Do you ever get an anxious feeling ... followed by a fearful thought that something must be going wrong?

Then the thought that something is wrong makes you feel more intense anxiety ... which makes you believe the fearful thought even more?

Maybe you start repeating this thought to yourself, or elaborating the fearful scenario with additional fearful thoughts. Of course, each one intensifies the anxiety, generating another fearful thought, and, in an instant, you're spiraling into a dark hole of fearful thoughts and anxious feelings.

This is how we double down on our anxiety. Like a compulsive gambler trying recoup his losses, we keep betting "double or nothing" over and over again. Of course, it never works—we just dive deeper into the dark. It's very stressful and depressing!

If you're like me, you'd like to end this painful, enervating spiral of dread and immunize yourself against it. Well, you can do it! Here's how:

1. *Recognize* that an unpleasant emotion doesn't mean there is something wrong with you or with the world.

2. Take a deep breath, and *breathe* into that feeling with a willingness to *just feel it*.

3. Look at the *thought* you're having about that feeling.

4. Instead of *believing* this fearful thought or trying to *block* it, simply think, "Do I really *have* to believe this thought?"

5. Now, look at the thought *again*. This thought may be about a specific situation that you wouldn't want to happen. That's only a *possibility*—not a belief. The problem thought that you *really* want to examine here is the one that tells you that if this dreaded thing happens that you don't want to happen, it means there is something wrong with you or with the world.

6. *Look* at that thought. Do you *have* to believe it? Never! Breathe deeply and easily. Relax. No spiral.

For some people, it isn't so easy to recognize that they don't have to believe the fearful thought.

Keeping this in mind, practice the steps again and change the last few steps just slightly. Notice how these steps enhance your inquiry:

• Recognize that an unpleasant emotion doesn't mean there is something wrong with you or with the world.

• Take a deep breath, and breathe into the feeling with a willingness to just feel it.

• Look at the thought you're having about the feeling.

• Instead of believing the fearful thought or trying to block it, simply think, "If I believe this fearful thought, I will feel more afraid. In fact, if anyone were to believe this fearful thought, they would feel afraid. So, this proves that I work perfectly.

There is nothing wrong with me. Having this feeling doesn't mean there is something wrong with me or with the world."

- Breathe. Relax. Look around. Look at your mind, thinking, "I work perfectly, even if I'm having a painful feeling. I'm perfectly okay, and I have a right to be kind and encouraging to myself."

- Look at this fresh thought of encouragement. Relax. No spiral.

I want to tell you a story now. It's an example of how quickly and easily you can dissolve a chronic, anxious problem state by inquiring into and challenging the thought process that creates it and keeps it going.

I had an adult client who spiraled into anxiety whenever she remembered a scary dream from her childhood. One night at about age 4, she "woke up" in the middle of her dream to find that a troll was sitting by her bed and a magic hat was sitting on her bedside table. She screamed...and the troll and the magic hat disappeared. Then she woke up (for real this time). For decades, she told me, she had been haunted by the fear of being harmed by this troll she had seen in her dream state.

I asked her to breathe and relax.

Then I pointed out to her that she was keeping this fear alive by the thoughts she was creating and believing. To illustrate, I listed a few of these thoughts:

1. You believe that trolls are bad. If something such as a troll is new or unfamiliar, you believe it must be bad.

2. You believe the troll wanted to hurt you and that you were powerless to stop him.

3. You believe that sooner or later it is going to happen—that the troll is going to "get you"—and therefore you have suffered with this anxiety for decades.

These views gave her pause, so I waited a few moments to let them sink in. Then I asked her to look at and *directly challenge* the thought that "trolls are bad" by asking herself, "Do I *have* to believe that?"

To help her arrive at disbelief, I asked her to consider a few possible scenarios:

1. You were a sleeping small child when you had that nightmare. If the troll had really wanted to hurt you, he probably could have done that before you woke up.

2. The troll disappeared with the hat when you screamed. He didn't try to muffle your scream and hurt you.

3. Maybe the troll had come to play with you. Maybe that's what the magic hat was for!

4. Maybe the troll left when you screamed and never came back because he cared about you and didn't want to upset you.

My client was able to accept this alternate interpretation of the "facts" and the anxiety left her. These interpretations just made much more sense! With a little calm examination and broadening of our perspective on "the facts," we can indeed immunize ourselves against imaginary fears—and all fears are imaginary! (Note that the instinctive flight-or-fight response is not a psychological fear.)

If you practice the steps I gave you, I'm sure you'll discover you can quickly overcome the habit of spiraling into anxiety.

I'm also sure that you'll find that questioning your thoughts is a surprisingly enjoyable and liberating exercise. Challenging your thoughts sharpens your mind and energizes you. You quickly learn the different situations in which you have been allowing many ridiculous thoughts to rob you of your good nature. With the clarity that comes from recognizing these thoughts for what they are, humor arises.

As soon as you see how absurd these thoughts are, they leave you!

If you would like to experience an in-depth presentation of how you can develop your own sharpness of mind to defeat fearful imagining, my video training *The Art and Skill of Therapeutic Inquiry* will give you that. This program is suitable for laypeople as well as therapists who can use it to earn CEUs. Upon completion, you'll be awarded a Certificate of Completion from the Institute for Therapeutic Learning. This training program is available now in the Finding True Magic online shop at shop.findingtruemagic.com.

2

Anger, Hurt, Loneliness, Shyness, and Feeling like a Failure

How to Throw Away
Hurt Feelings
So They Don't Come Back

....

IF WE FEEL UPSET WHEN things go wrong or something unpleasant and unexpected happens, we're not exactly unique in this world. On the other hand, if we develop the habit of holding on to these upset feelings, we may end up resorting to drinking too much, using addictive drugs, or overeating (using food as a drug) in a futile effort to try to feel better.

We usually don't even realize when we're being oversensitive or overreacting. As my wife sweetly says to me when I overreact, "You're a delicate flower, sweetheart." When I examine my upsets, I notice that I'm often acting as if I'm walking on a tightrope. Looking at my life in this distorted frame of reference, it make sense to react to mishaps as if the slightest disruption of our plan means we'll fall into a chasm. You yourself may have experienced something similar. Road rage, anyone?

Most of the time when things go wrong, it's really not a personal threat. What if we paused for a moment, took a deep breath, and clearly noticed that? It would be so much easier to deal with small mishaps, disappointments, and changes of plan. So, when plans change and I feel myself tightening up, I remind myself on the spot: "It's not personal." Interestingly, this helps me to relax!

Of course, our long-held fears and resentments are a bigger challenge. Renowned psychiatrist and medical hypnotist Milton Erickson advised his children that when someone hurt their feelings, they should run to the nearest garbage can and throw their hurt feelings into it. When I first heard this story many years ago, I thought, "That's silly and shocking advice—easier said than done! How would his kids be able to do that?" But the story stayed with me: How nice it would be to do that with my own hurt feelings, fears, and resentments. That method actually does work quite well and quite easily, although it took a while for me to figure that out. Here's what I discovered.

Once the deluded notion of personal threat is out of the way, the process is simple. Some people can just do it mentally, with enough emotional engagement to actually create a shift right on the spot: "Throw my hurt feeling in the garbage can...okay. Done!"

If you're a tough case like me, however, you may find that you need to physically act out the "throwing away" to engage enough emotional energy to effect positive change. Remember that you can throw away the hurt feelings. Remember, too, that holding on to anger and other kinds of emotional turmoil only hurts you. This will motivate you to make the effort to let go of these hurt feelings! You can train yourself to do this in a way that will work...every single time.

HERE'S HOW TO THROW AWAY HURT FEELINGS AND FORGET THEM

1. Stop, take a deep breath, and look at the upsetting emotion and the story that goes with it.

2. Hold your fists at heart or gut level, and then squeeze them to correspond to your inner struggle.

3. Visualize a garbage can in front of you—the special kind that disposes of emotional turmoil.

4. With both hands, *throw* the problem into the trash. Repeat this several times if there is any residue. Acting this out phys-

ically will increase your ability to create a genuine release so that later you can just do it mentally, on the spot.

5. Each time you throw some of your emotional turmoil away, take a deep, full breath.

6. Then turn around and step away from the trash can. Stand in an upright posture with your arms open and raised. Breathe in deeply, and smile!

7. In this relaxed, happy state, think of a few things that you're grateful for—this will intentionally enrich your relaxed, happy state with positive memories.

8. Now, while you're still holding on to this good state of mind, think about the original emotionally triggering event while choosing to keep your positive state. If even a quiver of the turmoil arises, just flick it into the garbage can with a smile.

Neuroscience has shown that upsetting memories are vulnerable to change when they are being retrieved. According to this science, your brain will be on your side and open to a positive shift when you practice this method!

Most of us learn to carry around hurt feelings while growing up as part of our family dynamics. If this happened for you, you may want to check out my online course, *Family Matters: 5 Ways to Stop Your Past from Screwing Up Your Future*, to free yourself from any limiting patterns you picked up as a child. It will help you throw old hurt feelings into the garbage can and forget about them for good!

Why It's Important to Keep Your Sense of Humor

....

IT'S NOT TOO HARD to see why it's essential to keep your sense of humor. When you're in a humorous state of mind, you feel good. And feeling good helps you with everything!

You can probably remember a time when sharing a joke with friends or laughing at yourself for something silly you did or said immediately lightened the mood of the moment. Humor relaxes us and helps us let go of unnecessary seriousness.

Your sense of humor is a natural aspect of your aliveness. It's not something you have to crank up. A humorous comment can shift an argument in an instant. In one moment of humor, you can instantly snap out of a dark mental state. This is because the essence of humor is the unrestricted flow of our living being. So, it's not surprising that sharing humor and laughter is also good for your health.

SOME OF THE HEALTH BENEFITS OF A SENSE OF HUMOR

1. We can think more clearly and creatively.

2. We are more willing to collaborate with respect and encouragement.

3. Laughter is good medicine! It not only reduces stress but it also strengthens our immune system, protects the heart, and improves digestion.

Whenever we think about anything, we create stories of varying intensity. "He's not listening to me!" or "Why does she always say something negative?" We tend to get trapped in these stories because they make us forget the constant, spacious, and spontaneous flow of being. A humorous comment can puncture the wall of an all-too-serious story or dismantle it altogether. Then we laugh. We take deep breaths. We relax. And most importantly, we come back to the felt sense of our humanity, our soft and compassionate human heart.

When we understand these positive effects of humor, we recognize that humor is a special kind of wisdom. When we're enjoying humor, there is nothing to cling tightly to, nothing to get trapped in. Humor doesn't have to be a joke that results in a big belly laugh. It can simply be a humorous reframe at a difficult time. If we suffer a great loss, a sense of humor saves us from a "poor me" mentality and enables us to suffer uprightly with tenderness, kindness, and clarity. Humor is the essential strength of fearless, healthy grieving.

Feeling good, light-hearted, and humorous is a sign that you're not in a conflicted or anxious state, at least for that moment. When we're not conflicted, our life energy is free to flow naturally. As any yoga instructor, dancer, or Olympic athlete will tell you, free-flowing energy feels good. Humor is flow. You simply cannot create a rigid, conflicted state of mind while you're actively flowing in relationship to yourself and others. Think of this flow of humor as enjoying riding on the breath of life. Moment by moment, wave upon wave.

Think back to the last time you were in humorous mental state. You were free. You weren't clinging to your beliefs about how things are or how you wanted them to be. And you weren't worried about how you looked to others. Letting ourselves experience this state of freedom on a regular basis is an act of kindness to ourselves and to others too, because when we let down our seriousness, our good-hearted humor can be communicated. And when we display good humor, it gives others permission to do the same.

Good humor is always a loving energy and it always feels good to share it. Humor is loving kindness in action.

If we think that a sense of humor is a "thing" that we have to search for or create, we may have a hard time connecting with humor when we need it most. If we're being genuine and relaxed with ourselves, we easily embody life's essentially humorous and joyful nature.

HERE ARE 6 STEPS TO RECONNECTING WITH YOUR SENSE OF HUMOR

1. Throughout the day, practice taking frequent moments to re-set yourself in your body. Just enjoy being presently relaxed, with a gentle smile. Practice enjoying being alive. Gratitude depends on enjoyment; we enjoy receiving the gift of life, and that inspires us to feel gratitude for it. Enjoyment and gratitude keep you at ease and build a vibrant capacity for you to respond to life with kind humor.

2. Then, to disrupt the "boxing in" quality of your thinking mind and any negative thoughts, practice "standing outside" yourself. Imagine you are a ball of awareness or light. Float outside of and all around your body. Look at your body's posture and your mental state from various angles as you float around it. Look with curiosity and affection, noticing whether "they" have forgotten to keep an affectionate regard for themselves. Radiate warmth and encouragement toward yourself.

3. Ask yourself, "Do they really need to hold on to this?" "Would anything bad happen if this person just smiled, stood up straight and at ease, exclaimed, 'Ha!' and then went about

their business with good cheer? After you answer this question, try saying a good strong "Ha!"

4. Notice the general tonality of any negative thoughts. Listen to these thoughts as if they're being spoken by a silly cartoon character with a funny, high-pitched voice.

5. When you notice a negative train of thought, ask, "Who is speaking to me this way?" Then imagine them standing on their head as they speak. (Make sure you're still imagining them speaking in their helium voice.)

6. Develop a habit of stopping and looking at your thoughts with a smile. Then take 3 deep, easy breaths, and stretch. Enjoy your body for a few seconds!

BUT ... WHAT IF YOU'RE EXPERIENCING INTENSE SUFFERING?

At times, you may be intensely suffering, as with a painful illness or deep grief. If this is happening for you, do not make light of your suffering in a mocking way. Have compassion for yourself. In the atmosphere of compassion, you can find little ways to lighten up and "get outside yourself." This is not a denial of your pain, it is a kindness to yourself. Remember, suffering with self-respect (not "poor me") is the wisdom of humor in action as you keep your heart soft and your kindness flowing.

A friend of mine told me about a time when he was in a state of intense physical pain. He began asking himself if any part of his body was free of pain. He discovered that his little toe was not in pain. Then he discovered his other toes were not in pain. Then he started congratulating each of his toes on not being in pain. Good for you! And you, and you, and you ... until he succeeded in entering a kind, humorous state even though he was in quite a lot of pain. He did this in a good-hearted way, free of any sense of sarcasm or ridicule.

Do we have anything to lose by developing an attitude that we are bigger than any challenge? The humorous, resilient aspect of our being makes this possible.

Do we have anything to lose by practicing smiling at fear and disappointment and renewing our spirit daily under any circumstances? The humorous aspect of our being is fearlessness and strength. It embodies the wisdom that *no obstacle* can remain in our way forever. Humor responds to obstacles with perseverance and without complaint.

Someone once asked the Dalai Lama how he could be so cheerful and kind and how he could laugh so much when his home country had been taken from him and thousands of his people had been killed. He replied that he couldn't stop them from taking everything away from him on the outside, but he clearly understood that it was his own choice and ability to keep his inner life rich and free and cheerful.

When we realize that no one else can take our inner life away from us without our agreement, we too can set an absolutely strong intention to cultivate a loving, happy heart every day, even in the midst of our challenges.

May you and all your toes experience great success!

How to Enjoy Letting Go of Anger and Other Inner Trolls in 4 Simple Steps

....

ANGER COMES FROM A creeping sense that we are small and somehow lacking. We're usually unconscious of this sense of smallness, but it makes us cling to what I call "Lower Self qualities." If we are to let go of these troublesome qualities, we need to be clear about what they are. Instead of just entertaining a general idea such as "I am now letting go of anger" or "I want to be in a higher state," we can have a list in mind. Below I've listed specific Higher and Lower Self qualities. Keeping these in mind makes it easier to identify our mood and shift our state when we get upset.

HIGHER SELF QUALITIES
Patience, kindness, empathy, compassion, courage, generosity, encouragement, and gentleness

LOWER SELF QUALITIES
Fearfulness, complaining, resenting, doubting, harshly judging, shaming, and blaming

I shared these lists with a client (let's call him Marcus) who had recently been challenged by a colleague. Marcus perceived his colleague as consistently blocking him from having something that held great personal importance for him. Marcus wanted to have a fruitful conversation with his colleague, and he needed to be at his very best when they met.

Of course, Marcus wanted to be in a good mental state. He wanted to choose certain Higher Self qualities to connect with. No argument there. But then I suggested to Marcus that he'd be in a more powerful state if he also envisioned—even prayed for—the other person to connect with Higher Self qualities as well. Initially, Marcus resisted. Very quickly, though, he realized it was silly to wish for Higher Self qualities for himself while holding onto a bad opinion of someone else. That holding on was clearly based on fear, blame, and resentment—all Lower Self qualities. We had a good laugh about having a low opinion of someone while trying to get into a loving and generous state. How high can you really go if you still believe that others are low?

Now, when I use the word "pray," I'm not suggesting that a belief in God is required. Praying doesn't require an entity or an object that you pray to. The power of prayer lies in focusing our attention on a positive concept or vision. You could just as easily say that you can bless others by holding positive thoughts about them, which includes imagining their well-being.

Here's an important tip:

You can use this when you're facing someone you're angry at, or when you're speaking to someone you've been holding a resentment against. If you want to *truly transform* your inner state from anger to resourcefulness, then change your vision of yourself, as well as your vision of the other person. Imagine the situation developing into a positive outcome for *everyone involved.*

As he considered this viewpoint, Marcus became willing to pray for his "adversary" as well as for himself. Then I asked him to wholeheartedly envision himself manifesting the Higher Self qualities of his choice. Suddenly, Marcus said he felt imposed upon. The word "wholeheartedly" had triggered a sense of some impossible performance standard that he couldn't live up to.

I quickly remembered that I had once had a similar response

upon hearing this word. I had also worked with clients who had reacted negatively to the words "persistent" and "constant." Spiritual instructions often include these words: "pray constantly," "make wholehearted effort," and "be persistent in your remembrance of the sacredness of all beings." I remembered that I had once become very discouraged hearing such instructions. Like Marcus, I was taking them as admonitions to meet an impossible standard of perfection.

Then one of my teachers explained that to be wholehearted, constant, or persistent doesn't mean attaining perfection. I shared this clarification with Marcus. I told him that to do anything wholeheartedly simply means making a concerted, focused effort.

I encouraged Marcus to try imagining the best for himself and his challenging colleague for just 5 minutes a day. After that, he could relax and let go. The key would be to do this daily for at least 5 minutes, and if he could do it in the same place and at the same time, even better. But then he should just relax and let it go. "If your affirmation or object of contemplation returns to your mind during the day," I told Marcus, "that's fine. But you don't have to try to hold on to it every minute." After hearing this explanation, he felt much better and decided to give it a try.

Marcus did this for a few days before he met with his "adversary." On the day of the meeting, he noticed with surprise that the man smiled when he saw Marcus approaching. The conversation proceeded with ease, and both men clearly enjoyed each other's company. Marcus told me, "I guess what happens on the inside really does determine what happens on the outside!"

4 STEPS FOR INVITING A HIGHER SELF QUALITY INTO YOUR LIFE

So, here's your invitation: Pick a short affirmation such as "I am healthy and happy," or "I succeed with grace and ease," or whatever works for you. Consider the list of Higher Self qualities:

patience, kindness, empathy, compassion, courage, generosity, encouragement, and gentleness.

Choose 1 quality that you wish to be planted within you and grow, and apply these 4 steps:

1. Make your statement short and positive.

2. Don't be concerned about it being "true."

3. Repeat your statement for 5 minutes, *not 15 seconds*. Try this daily for 1 month, just for 5 minutes, and then let it go. But do it daily!

4. Enjoy the results.

Have an exuberant day, every day! (Hey, that could be your affirmation!)

Overcoming Loneliness and Shyness: 7 Messages of Self-Respect

....

"I'M LONELY. I WOULD be interested in dating, but I'm just too shy for that." I feel a pang of sadness when I hear people talk about how lonely they feel and how shyness stops them from enjoying this important and highly enjoyable aspect of life—the joy of genuine human connection.

It has been a while since I was actively looking into dating, or even making new friends, but I know the importance of human connection and affection. I depend on my strong ties with family and community and fortunately, at those times when I need moral support, encouragement, and companionship, someone is usually there to listen and care. When someone I love is patient with my rough edges, it's easier to get past them. And when my wife shares the delight I feel in our granddaughter's antics, it doubles my joy.

Connecting with others gives life its pizzazz! It is relaxing to feel that another person sees and hears and understands you, or is at least making a sincere effort to understand, which often feels just as good. So, what is happening when we feel we cannot make genuine human connections? Could it have something to do with our thinking?

When I talk with people who are thinking about dating or making friends, I hear a variety of common complaints:

"Everyone is staring at their phone."

"Millennials would rather play remote video games with one another than meet up in person."

"Dating sites are a hassle. People misrepresent themselves. It is hard to tell if someone is going to be interesting, or even safe."

All of these may be valid observations, but in themselves, they are **not** the root cause of the difficulty we tend to have with meeting new people. What **is** the root cause of loneliness and shyness, then? It's fear.

Sometimes it's understandable to be afraid. We shy away from exposing ourselves yet again—what if it doesn't pay off? Never mind bad relationships, even a bad date or an argument can leave us feeling wounded and stuck. We may start withdrawing a little, hiding out and lying low after a crappy experience with an ex, only to realize later that years have passed and we're still spending a surprising amount of our free time alone streaming videos and eating ice cream. At that point, our shyness has claimed our evenings and weekends. Where would we find time for another person? We may be lonely, but shyness (a code name for fear) is now making our decisions.

When we focus on our fearful beliefs ("Maybe I'm just meant to be alone" or "Maybe I'm not interesting or lovable"), we generate even more fear. We make it very scary for ourselves to overcome loneliness and shyness.

Let's break this down. How does it happen, exactly?

When we focus again and again on feelings of fear and a belief in our shyness, we replay the stories that go with these feelings. It's like we're staring at a GIF of ourselves frightened and failing, a never-ending video loop of doom. This gives our brain a powerful message:

"This is reality."

Our brain is a gullible sort.

Unfortunately, we tend to take our brain's conclusions at face value. So, when our gullible brain repeatedly presents us with a barrage of "ads" depicting us in a fearful state of shyness, we decide that this is a permanent hopeless condition, that "this is us." We believe more and more strongly that we're incapable of creating and maintaining connections with others.

7 MESSAGES FOR OVERCOMING LONELINESS AND SHYNESS
You can change how you talk to yourself! Self-talk is just thinking, and most of our thoughts are only arbitrary judgments, not laws of the universe. By thinking these 7 new thoughts on a regular basis, you can get your brain to show you "ads" that help you enjoy a better, kinder life. And when you're enjoying life, others take notice—connections come easily and naturally.

1. **"I am an amazing creation of life itself, equal to every other being."** Every being on Earth is an expression of sacred living energy and consciousness, regardless of its appearance or abilities. Self-love and self-respect, as well as simple gratitude for the miracle of life, have a way of revealing and radiating beauty in a person, regardless of their form, their age, or any other attributes.

2. **"I deserve respect and encouragement."** To begin practicing kind and encouraging self-talk, it helps to look at how you think about yourself and how you talk to yourself. You may discover you're putting yourself down more than you ever suspected. You may see more clearly how often you're tricking yourself into believing that you're "not good enough to interest anyone" and that "there is no one out there anyway." It can be a great exercise to write down your self-judgments. That way you can look at each one before it vaporizes and is replaced by the next one. Then you can have a great time creating self-encouraging and self-respecting statements and repeating those messages to yourself instead.

3. **"Even though** ... *[Fill in the blank with any negative put-down thought]* ... **nevertheless, I love and respect myself thorough-**

ly and completely, as a mysterious creation of life itself." This is a useful template for applying kind, encouraging thoughts in an unstoppable way! Whatever judgments, temporary feeling states, or "special conditions" arise that your brain cooks up, keep insisting. Just repeatedly affirm that you love and accept yourself regardless of any conditions. Don't struggle with your negative thoughts. Agree with them and build on them. You can be tricky, too!

4. **"Hmm, thanks for sharing. You could be right about that. Nevertheless, I love and respect myself thoroughly and completely, as a mysterious creation of life itself."** Affirm this positive truth in the face of any fearful or negative thoughts that come up. Don't fight with or struggle with negative thoughts. Relax as best you can and smile at them as you think this. To make it even more interesting, think this thought while smiling into a mirror.

5. **"I enjoy my own good company."** There's real magic in this one. First, realize that you are never really alone because you are always "with yourself." As you practice relating to yourself with more kindness, interest, and encouragement to enjoy your unique gift of life, you become less and less concerned with others' judgments, real or imagined. Your own judgments of others dissolve too, as you replace them with kind, encouraging thoughts. You realize that your shyness was a result of self-rejecting beliefs that others trained you to think when you were too young to know any better. Seeing through this false programming more and more, you're happy to enjoy the good company of others when it happens, but you're not particularly concerned about being alone or with others. You are becoming your own good company more and more vibrantly every day.

6. **"I am happy with myself."** When you are happy with your-self—in other words, happy with the mystery of life that cre-ates us all—you are no longer struggling to be happy with a false self. You gradually let go of this false self altogether be-cause you see it for what it is: nothing more than a high-main-tenance collection of ego-judgments needing constant justi-fication just to stay afloat. You're happy with your real self, which means you can relax and enjoy the gift of life that is effortlessly arising as "you"—breath by breath, heartbeat by heartbeat.

7. **"I have unlimited kindness to give."** You've heard of med-itation, right? This is the real meditation. It is not a struggle to create some goodness in yourself. Nor is it a big effort to attain some super-spiritual state of consciousness. Cultivating kindness toward, interest in, and respect for your freely given, living consciousness moment by moment is perfect nourish-ment and support. You are enjoying a natural state of giving. "Free kindness for all! Here you go." No strings, no condem-nations attached. You don't have to "do" anything, and others don't have to do anything either. As you see yourself and oth-ers more and more from this perspective of "free kindness," you realize that all of us are receiving the same gift—life, giv-en freely. Reveling in this gift, you begin to enjoy exploring ways to relate to our shared humanness together.

Enjoy the gift!

Feeling Like a Failure:
The Oldest Con There Is

RECENTLY A FRIEND SAID to me, "I feel like my family sees me as a failure. Do you have any suggestions?"

My answer may have sounded blunt, but I said, "If they're not being respectful and encouraging to you, then why even care what they think?!"

Many adults struggle with this problem. Simply because we're walking around in a grownup body, we mistakenly think we are dealing with an adult problem with our adult mind. But actually, whether it takes the form of a mild concern or harsh self-criticism, worrying about others' disapproval is not an adult concern. It originates with our childhood conditioning.

When we are little children, especially before the age of 7, it is natural for us to want to constantly feel love, approval, and encouragement from our parents.

During this developmental period, it's important for children to receive unconditional warmth and loving support, even when we do things "wrong." Receiving such encouragement helps us build a strong sense of inner strength and self-esteem. We internalize the warmth we receive from our parents or other caregivers. We also internalize an attitude of confidence that we can handle whatever life presents. The child reasons, "If they have confidence in me, I'm going to have confidence in myself." This is the great gift that parents give their children when they're able to offer encouragement in most any situation—especially when a child makes a big mistake.

Let's say a child breaks their mother's favorite vase. Can she honestly express her sadness to the child and at the same time direct kindness toward them? If she knows how to do this, the child learns an invaluable lesson about how to keep a heart connection to another person, even when you're upset by that person's actions: "Oh, sweetheart, that must have really scared you when the vase smashed to the floor. Mommy loved that vase and is sad that it's broken. But Mommy loves you so much more and is happy you didn't get hurt."

SELF-ATTACK OR ENCOURAGEMENT: OUR INTERNALIZED MESSAGES

Around the age of 7, we discover our emerging cognitive faculties. We begin to explore the world with this newfound "mind" that has the ability to reason and evaluate. This new mind is filled with evaluations of ourselves and our abilities. Where did these come from? We have internalized them from our first 7 years of life, merely by paying attention to the way our parents or caregivers regarded us and communicated with us.

When a child's mind is filled with internalized messages of loving encouragement from those times when they "failed" to do things "right," those messages immunize the child against self-attacking thoughts and worries that they are somehow "not good enough." Such children find it easy to be kind and encouraging to others, especially if they see other children struggling. It literally pains them to see someone feeling bad about themselves.

But even the most well-meaning parents or caregivers can make the error of regarding a child's "mistakes" with irritation instead of understanding. In those cases, they may have ignored, punished, and ridiculed us for things we did that they believed were "wrong." And they also may have intimidated us into doing what they considered "right." When this happened, we internalized the message that we ourselves, not just our actions, were somehow flawed or "not good enough." The effect is worse if the message is delivered to a child consistently. Then the child reasons, "I can't do things well enough to deserve love, warmth, and encouragement."

The sad result is that the child internalizes a general sense of hopelessness. Once we have internalized this message, we repeat it to ourselves. It is as though we have been conned! We have fallen for the idea that love is to be earned. We believe that we will only be loved if we do things "right"—if we "succeed."

If a child is given messages of disapproval—if love was withheld when they "failed" to please a parent or caregiver—then the child's newly emerging mind is infected with fear, doubt, and self-attacking thoughts. Consequently, such children are quick to attack others even as they grow to adulthood, believing that attacks and intimidation are "normal" behavior. If our mind has developed this way, we actually feel better about ourselves if we see someone else as "less than." It's a sad state of affairs all around.

The point here, of course, is not that we should blame or attack our parents if they weren't able to give us unconditional, loving encouragement. Like all parents and caregivers, ours did the best they could, based on their own less-than-perfect upbringing. The point is that we have the power to free ourselves from any unnecessary fearful concerns that were passed on to us by others.

Taking a look at the signs below can help us see when we're operating in "fearful child" consciousness versus when we're operating in true adult consciousness. And remember: Nothing is permanent. As we begin to pay attention to what's going through our mind and as we recognize any "fearful child" attitude, we reclaim the power to direct our mind to true adult consciousness. We can pause and give ourselves a message of loving encouragement.

6 SIGNS THAT WE ARE OPERATING IN
FEARFUL CHILD CONSCIOUSNESS

1. We are worried about what others think of us.

2. We believe our performance in the world determines our worth as a being.

3. We have an emotionally volatile inner life.

4. We believe in and we fear rejection. We believe that if someone rejects us, it proves that we are not good enough.

5. We are so absorbed in the drama of these concerns that we lose touch with a sense of gratitude for the gift of life and its mysterious beauty.

6. We have an unrecognized attitude of immortality. We don't notice when we're assuming that we have all the time in the world to waste on petty resentments, regrets, jealousies, and fearful, dog-eat-dog ambitions.

6 SIGNS THAT WE ARE OPERATING IN
TRUE ADULT CONSCIOUSNESS

1. We cultivate and preserve our self-respect and integrity by relating to ourselves and others with kindness and respect for our shared humanity.

2. We are clear that our value as a mysterious living being cannot be diminished by our "failures"—nor can it be improved by our "successes." We don't elevate or diminish others based on their "successes" and "failures." We just don't think in those terms. We want everyone to flourish and feel their worth.

3. Our inner life is serene … because we are not afraid of judgment in the realm of success or failure. We regard life as a learning curve. Ideas of success and failure are unhelpful, shaming labels that harm us in our journey and our learning process of living.

4. We are clear that when someone rejects us, they do so based on their own inner turmoil. We understand that they are rejecting their idea of us, which is always based on their fearful rejection of an idea of themselves that was formed in their childhood.

5. We realize, moment by moment, that life is a gift … and we enjoy the felt sense of being alive. This felt sense includes the poignant, sweet heartbreak of knowing the fragile and temporary nature of everyone and everything. Our natural response to this is to extend kindness and encouragement.

6. We are keenly aware of our mortality while feeling ever-new gratitude and astonishment that anything at all exists! Our sense of gratitude at the wonder of life protects us from the influence of fearful, morbid notions of life being pointless because it will one day end.

From these descriptions, you can see that being afraid of being judged a failure by our family or anyone else is actually a helpful sign! It simply shows us that we're missing appreciation and respect for the miracle of our life. What does this mean for the future?

It is an invitation to enjoy traveling the learning curve. There's no need to be down on yourself at all. Very few of us had perfect parents. Most of us have to do this work on ourselves at some point or another. You can have a great time watching your mind and developing the insights and qualities of True Adult Consciousness. Good luck! You are worth it!

3

Befriending Yourself and Other Things Couples Need to Know

How to Be
a Good Friend
to Yourself

SOMEONE ASKED ME RECENTLY, "You say it's important to be friends with yourself. How can I do that?"

Are you friendly to anybody? Well, it's the same way with yourself. You're a person just like they are. When you see somebody, do you smile and say, "Hi, how are you doing?" So, in the morning when you look in the mirror, you can say, "Hi, how are you doing? I love you. I hope you have a good day." And practice meaning it.

Being friends with ourselves is the same thing as being friendly to anybody else.

Once you realize that being your own best friend requires the same kind of attention and effort as being a friend to someone else, you have cleared an astonishing hurdle. It's astonishing because it doesn't occur to so many of us that we're people just like everyone else! We readily recognize that others deserve loving care and kindness, but somehow it doesn't occur to us that we ourselves deserve exactly those same things.

For most of us, this is a blind spot that develops in childhood. As children, we have a natural developmental gullibility. You can make a child believe anything from the myth of Santa Claus to the idea that they don't deserve love and respect because they spilled their milk or wet their pants. Every spank or harsh glare from an adult communicates to a young child in a profound way that they are not good enough to receive love and kindness.

All of us as children are conditioned, in varying degrees of intensity, by this sort of treatment (and worse) to develop this *blind spot* about our own *precious worthiness as a living being.*

That blind-spot conditioning taught us that our thoughts, feelings, speech, actions, and appearance were somehow defective and irredeemable. No wonder so many of us act meek and try to disappear. Or become rageful or depressed in reaction to the pressure of pent-up pain at this horrific insult to our being.

The blind spot (our sense of unworthiness) is maintained by our belief. We accept and believe the thoughts and feelings we first experienced as children: "Daddy yelled at me loudly for a long time when I spilled the milk. I feel so, so sad. He must not love me."

Later, as teens and adults, we continue to maintain this blind spot. We not only believe these thoughts and feelings but we also conclude that they are uniquely ours and therefore prove something about us personally. But, they are not ours—they are simply human thoughts and feelings experienced by everyone. Therefore, they cannot prove anything about any one of us specifically. There is no shame in experiencing any thought or feeling. There is nothing you can think or feel that would mean anything about you personally, nothing that could set you apart from all of humanity.

When we talk about "actions" here, we are referring to human actions that can be mistaken and even harmful. But mistaken and harmful actions do not cause our being to become bad. These actions only indicate that we need education and support to understand which of them are genuinely helpful and which ones are not helpful.

5 WAYS TO PRACTICE BEING YOUR OWN BEST FRIEND
You can practice these 5 simple, yet powerfully healing actions that can dissolve your blind spot (that sense of unworthiness). This way, you can develop the habit of being your own best friend.

1. **Remind yourself frequently that you are having a human experience and that no aspect of it is proof of your unworthiness.** You can't experience any feeling that is uniquely yours, separate from your humanness. We are all in the same boat!

2. **Practice relaxing and extending kindness to yourself often throughout the day.** Stop and put your hands over your heart in a caring way. Focus on the tenderness and warmth of your skin. Feel the movement of your breath.

3. **Reflect on the wonder of your existence.** Notice that life is manifesting you. You are life's gift to yourself and to the world. Life wants you to thrive. Life wants everything it manifests to thrive. Life is loving you into existence breath by breath, heartbeat by heartbeat. Relax and open your heart to this gift as best you can—no judgment!

4. **Smile at yourself in the mirror.** At first, you may feel uncomfortable doing this. It may even intensify your feelings of self-rejection when you go against them by extending kindness to yourself. Keep practicing anyway, with a genuine, warm smile. It is natural to appreciate that miraculous manifestation of life you see in the mirror—you! That appreciation is your support. Stay inspired by remembering that self-rejection was something you were tricked into when you were a child. You may find that it builds your sense of determination to think that, through this practice, you're rescuing and healing that child self so it can grow up and merge into your fully present adult self. Smile at the child, too.

5. **Program your smartphone to send you this message: "No matter what I have ever thought, said, done, or experienced, I deserve love and respect as much as anyone."** Then take a

moment to give some love and respect to yourself. Just open up a bit and kindly breathe in.

(Sending a text message to yourself is as easy as texting a friend. Just create a new blank message and enter your own phone number in the **To:** field. And if you find yourself using this method often, you can add yourself to your list of contacts.)

These simple exercises and contemplations are more than enough to guide you into a state of loving "self-friendship." The key to being a good friend to yourself is to repeat these actions often, every day, until they become powerful and habitual—healthy loving habits. Recognize this as a joyful healing assignment. Good luck and enjoy!

Why Mindfulness in Relationships Helps You Make Better Choices

···

A COUPLE CAME TO see me once, and they were very grumpy with each other. They'd had a big fight the previous week, and it was so bad that the woman's husband had actually packed his bags and was ready to go out the door. I said, "Wow! What was the fight about?" The husband explained, "I was in the kitchen making a meal, looking forward to sharing it with my wife when she got home. But when she came in the door, she immediately started criticizing me, saying that the kitchen counter was really dirty."

At this point, his wife broke in. "It was! It was filthy. I came home from a hard day's work looking forward to a nice meal, and the first thing I see is this filthy countertop, and I know I'm probably going to be the one who has to clean it up. So I gave him a piece of my mind. And he lost it! He just got angrier and angrier and started packing his bags, saying that all I ever do is criticize him and things like that."

I thanked them both for somehow surviving that moment with their marriage intact. She had been able to calm her husband down and keep him from leaving the house by apologizing. But it was obvious that both of them still feared repeating this kind of fight because they both believed there would be another dirty countertop in their future. So I applauded them on reconciling and invited them to take a closer look at the situation. I suggested that they might look at aspects of this experience from a new perspective that would dispel their fear of another *kitchen-crumb crisis*.

That's how we got onto the subject of mindfulness. Not just *any* old mindfulness, but the most *important* kind, and how they could use it to bring their relationships to a whole new level of loving awareness.

WHAT IS THE MOST IMPORTANT KIND OF MINDFULNESS?

Mindfulness is not just a technique—it is a saving grace in all of our relationships. We talk about being mindful of our breath, of how we cut the carrots, of our posture. But the most important way we can practice mindfulness in relationships (or in any other area of life) is by being mindful that what we're experiencing is *not a solid reality*. It's an experience that we *construct* all day long, moment by moment.

You can't be mindful of what something *isn't*. In order to understand that reality isn't solid, you need to be mindful of what your everyday, *apparently* solid reality actually **is**. It doesn't help to lecture and convince yourself into thinking that this world isn't real and that everything's an illusion. That's only adopting a belief. We exert *mindfulness* so that we can see the way things actually *are*, beyond our beliefs about them. So, if our reality isn't solid, then what is it?

REALITY: A Case Study

To do a case study of reality, we have to understand **5 kinds of choices** we are constantly making. These choices determine our experience of life every single day.

Choice 1: What We're *Focusing* On

The couple who came to see me after their fight were very focused on that dirty kitchen countertop. Even while they were telling the story to me in my office, they were fixating on the crumbs and grease! In this way, the dirty countertop had become a solid reality for them—a reality they were carrying around with them from place to place.

Choice 2: What We're *Overlooking* in Our Environment (Our *Inner* Environment as Well as Our *Outer* Environment)

At that point, I circled my finger around the corner of my desktop and asked the husband, "What do you think would have happened if you had drawn her attention to a *clean* area of the countertop and said to her, 'But honey, look how nice *this part* looks!"? They laughed. Then I ran my finger along the side of my desk and said, "And honey, look how clean *this part* of the cabinet is!" Then they really cracked up.

Choice 3: The *Value* We're Giving to the Things We Notice

Pointing out these silly examples helped the couple notice that (a) they had a choice about what to focus on, and (b) they had a choice about what to give importance to. They got a powerful look at how *dramatically* our experience can *change* when we exercise our power to make these choices consciously, instead of reacting to what seems to be a solid, unforgiving "reality."

Choice 4: The *Beliefs* We're Holding about How Things Work in the World

They began to appreciate the laughter and freedom of changing their perspective about external reality. In particular, the husband saw that he had been holding a *belief* (or internal reality) that if his wife said something critical, he was *required* to take it personally and feel bad about himself. Now he realized, with great good humor, that taking her words personally was an *entirely ridiculous* activity.

Choice 5: What We *Perceive* Our *Choices* to Be

I asked him to imagine walking over to his wife while she was complaining about the dirty countertop and giving her a big hug, looking her in the eyes and saying, "I'm so glad you got home safely. May I have this dance?" and sweeping her into a waltz.

They both found this image extremely delightful! We continued to play with other possible choices of things they could say and do in this situation. Soon they began to understand how important it is to stay mindful that better (and more enjoyable) choices are *always available to us*.

By practicing mindfulness, we remember more and more often that we hold the power—

- to *choose* what to focus on

- to *notice* what we may be overlooking (both inside and outside ourselves)

- to *change* the value we're placing on whatever we're noticing

- to *examine* the beliefs we're engaging, to see whether they fit

- to *set aside* our default reactions and look for better choices

With mindful awareness of all of these aspects of our experience, we can change any seemingly solid, irritating "reality" into an opportunity for playfulness and warmth. As you get better and better at practicing mindfulness in relationships, you'll find that you'll look at your life much more creatively. This creative, playful outlook will help you make better choices in every other area of your life as well!

How to Stop Worrying in Relationships

....

Do you ever find yourself worrying what your partner or spouse might be thinking of you? Is it hard for you to be open and honest because you're afraid they'll think you're stupid, dorky, or worse…boring? Maybe you've found yourself mentally revising and editing what you wanted to say to them, so much so that you got discouraged and gave up trying.

Wouldn't it be nice if you knew an easy way to escape from the painful struggle of second-guessing yourself? You can do it. (More on that in a moment.)

People often think that somehow they'll have to "do battle"— meaning that they'll have to somehow overpower their own mind in order to stop worrying about what others think. We may work very hard to try to defeat the harsh, judgmental thoughts in our minds. But when we try to defeat our own thoughts this way, we always lose. Ironically, by mobilizing the energy of all that struggle, we've actually strengthened our belief in our harsh self-judgments! Then we end up feeling like hopeless victims.

Here's how to quickly take back your freedom to live spontaneously, without fear of being judged by your spouse or partner:

1. **Recognize that when you fear judgment, you are imagining yourself as a person who can be judged**. In other words, you have an "idea of self" or an idea of who you are that can be critiqued.

The fact is, we can judge only our *idea* of ourselves, others, or our world. Judging is a thought process. So a "person being judged" in this thought process is just an *idea* we have. That thought isn't us, and it isn't anyone else either.

Look at it this way: If you were judging an actual *person*, then if they were to pass away, it would mean you couldn't judge them anymore. And of course, we know this isn't the case. This is because you were judging an *idea* of that person, *not* the actual person themselves. An *idea* can easily survive the death of an actual person.

Of course, you can agree with your judgment or with someone else's judgment. This agreement produces a strong emotion. We usually mistake strong emotion as proof that what we're thinking is true. But it's just a strong emotion—it doesn't mean that our judgment (our thought) is true.

In the same way, hearing someone voice a judgmental thought about you doesn't mean that your real self is being judged. If it bothers you, this simply means that you agree with the one judging you—you are both simply sharing the same opinion about an imaginary self (who isn't you)!

2. **Recognizing this will lead you to an even more wonderful discovery:** that there was never a possibility for you to be the target of ridicule or judgment, and there never could be. People can attack or judge only a self that's imaginary—a thought of self.

3. **Try this out for yourself**—try refusing to live in the trance of being only an imaginary self.

See what you find out!

The 3 Skills You Need
If You Want
to Help Others

....

MANY PEOPLE TRY TO make their mark on the world and establish their financial security before considering how to give back. Others feel a strong pull to dedicate themselves to service quite early in life.

When she was 16 years old, climate activist Greta Thunberg was nominated for the Nobel Peace Prize for her peaceful protests that sparked a movement among young people worldwide to raise awareness of the need for international leaders to unite in responding to climate change.

But however or whenever our aspiration to help others may arise, the most important thing is that we have a clear sense about how to do this skillfully.

HELPING OTHERS REQUIRES SKILL

What is the skill set that allows us to develop clarity about helping others? How can we engage in acts of kindness or service wisely so that our actions are truly effective?

Our entire planet is sustained through an intricate symphony of interdependent activity that provides constant help and support for the lives of us and all beings. Yet the art and skill of effectively offering help may be the most-often overlooked knowledge throughout human history.

First, we need to recognize how the law of cause and effect is operating—at all times!

When I first heard the saying, "The road to hell is paved with good intentions," I wondered how that could be the case. Later on, though, I learned 3 essential components to accomplishing any outcome, and suddenly this old saying made perfect sense.

THE 3 ESSENTIAL SKILLS TO BRING ABOUT A POSITIVE OUTCOME

Each of the elements I'm about to describe is essential to manifest any truly helpful result. Each is a skill, because each one requires thoughtful contemplation that clarifies the intention of your desired outcome, ensures that it is worth pursuing, and sets you on an effective course of action.

- **Skill 1: Pure motivation.** You have no competing agendas. You are simply, selflessly inspired to help. By not expecting any reward or accolade, your mind is clear and free to focus on how best to apply your energy and attention.

- **Skill 2: A worthy goal.** You are sure that what you intend to do will truly benefit yourself and others. You have looked into the issue and discovered how you can help to bring about this positive outcome.

  It looks like we're off to a very good start! It may even seem as though we already have all of the helpful elements we need. If you have a pure intention and a worthy goal, what could go wrong?

  But before we discuss Skill 3, let's step back for a moment.

  I live in Seattle. One day my heart swells with an inspiration to visit my oldest friend in New York City whom I haven't seen in decades. I contact him to suggest the visit, and soon we're both looking forward with joyful anticipation to reconnecting. So far, I have 2 of the 3 necessary components for accomplishing my goal of a friendly reunion.

I jump in my car and head off with unbridled enthusiasm. I'm so excited to see my old friend Anthony that I don't even notice I am taking the Interstate 5 South instead of Interstate 90 East. I continue blissfully driving in this direction and end up in Los Angeles, not in New York City. At that point, some might say I had driven into hell or at least into hellish traffic. But before we start debating whether the traffic is worse in LA or NYC, let's look at the *third essential element* for accomplishing a goal.

- **Skill 3: The Right Action.** You make the right choices, which depend on understanding the law of causality, of cause and effect. If I'm going to stay off the road to hell, my good intentions need to be mixed with skill and awareness.

So, how do we develop these essential skills?

A GOOD BEGINNING: 4 STEPS TO HELPING OTHERS

1. **Pick the proper seed of motivation.** Sometimes it can be quite a challenge to obtain the fruit or at least the helpful result that we want. Check to be sure the seed is good and that it really will grow the fruit you intend. Closely examine the information about this fruit you think you want. If we choose to grow a fruit we have never eaten before and think it is "good" based only on hearsay, we may get a big disappointment when we taste the real thing. Consider the cautionary tale of plastic bag bans, which inadvertently resulted in increased greenhouse gas emissions!

2. **Learn how to prepare the ground to encourage growth and fruition.** Before you begin trying to help, do your research. Consider how and when to plant your seed of motivation, how to protect and nurture it, and how to direct the growth

of the young sprout. How do we keep pests away from this new sprout without spreading toxins? How do we keep critters from nibbling at this immature tender plant?

3. **Check for signs of unintended consequences.** We thought our forests and adjacent farms would be safer and more peaceful for ourselves and the animals if we got rid of all the vicious wolves. But over a relatively short time, we saw our forests and animals become unhealthy. Reintroducing wolves that we once thought of as the source of the problem actually caused every aspect of the forests to flourish again, even restoring rivers!

4. **Cultivate a long-term awareness.** Events don't begin and end according to our arbitrary definitions. A long-term ecological perspective is essential to success in every area of life. I admire the Native Americans' way of making decisions, mindful of the effects of their actions on the next 7 generations to come. I have also heard that China is currently operating in accord with a 1,000-year plan, while America operates from one tweet to the next!

When we accomplish an outcome that truly succeeds in being helpful, it isn't magic. It is a direct result of our fulfillment of the *3 essential skills for helping others*: a good clear intention, a good goal, and good effectual action—as well as engaging skillfully with circumspect awareness, right from the beginning.

3 Things All Couples Need to Know to Improve Communication in Relationships

....

RECENTLY A COUPLE CAME to see me to try to solve a Very Unique Problem in their relationship: They weren't getting along. I'm kidding, of course. Most of the couples who end up in my office aren't getting along and want to improve communication in their relationship. Sometimes they're not even aware that there's a problem of communication in the relationship—they just think they're an unhappy couple and they want to be a happy one. That's a simple enough request to make of your hypnotherapist, isn't it?

So, what do I do?

When I'm working to help a couple communicate better, it may surprise you to hear that I don't employ the latest tricks to get men to understand women better, or vice versa, or any of that sort of thing. Improving relationship communication is actually much simpler than that—if the hypnotherapist's approach is transpersonal in nature.

As a transpersonal hypnotherapist, I've discovered that helping couples improve their communication is a matter of embodying (not merely believing) a simple, yet often elusive, perspective about the nature of our minds and our experiences.

What is this simple, yet elusive, perspective?

As a hypnotherapist, I do not have to put people in trance—they are already in trance. In fact, all of our problems are born of our trances. A therapist can use standard hypnotic processes (which I teach in my hypnotherapy certification course) in the same way that poisons are used in proper measure to make medicines.

But a transpersonal hypnotherapist practices this alchemy with the understanding that the goal is not to help clients become established in comfortable trances, but rather to be free of trances altogether! The goal is to be present, at ease, and free of fear—whole and peaceful. In order to help people become free of troubling trance states, I introduce *3 ideas* that everyone must understand before they can be truly happy in their relationships:

3 THINGS YOU MUST LEARN
BEFORE YOU CAN BE FREE AND HAPPY

1. **We are not who we think we are.** Who we think we are is our deepest trance state (actually a bundle of trance states). Knowing this makes it easier to relax and let go of all the thoughts and feelings we identify as being "ours." When you can do this, your communication is naturally more curious and open-minded. You ask more questions; you listen without thinking you already know what's about to be said. The whole process becomes less intense and much more interesting.

2. **To the degree that our awareness is absorbed in and identified with our thoughts, we live in a hypnotic state.** Most of us are accustomed to living within this tightly defined state rather than in a spontaneous "real" state, an "awake" state. Once you understand that there's an alternative—that you can respond to your experience as new in each moment, life becomes a great deal more surprising and delightful, and memories of the past don't create the fear and dread they once generated.

3. **All communication is a sharing of our hypnotic states, dream states, and even deluded states.** We share our hypnotic states in both intrapersonal and interpersonal communication to

the degree that we're sharing our thoughts about reality rather than a direct experience of reality.

When you say, "I feel you don't appreciate all that I do for you," you're talking about your hypnotic state, your ideas and thoughts. You're not talking about your feelings (sadness, disappointment, annoyance, and such) at all! But if you know that whatever you say to your partner is going to be an artifact of your customary hypnotic states, that makes it easier to see the discomfort of your negative feeling as an *object in awareness*. It's a fluid energy pattern, not some "thing" you must hold onto for dear life.

All day long (and even in our dreams), we are selectively attending to our ideas about ourselves in order to make choices that define and determine our lives. It's amazing how we can be doing this continuously and without even being aware of it, isn't it? And…

If the root idea of who we are is a mistake, then our whole accustomed process of strategizing to improve our lives is a mishap, with varying degrees of painful and pleasurable consequences.

Understanding these 3 perspectives, which strike at the root of our mistaken perceptions of ourselves and our experience, opens the possibility of complete freedom of thought, feeling, and perception in the moment.

If you're aware that your idea of "myself" is a set of ideas—a trance—then it's not such a big deal if your partner says, "You never listen to me! Why are you so selfish?!" You don't take it personally. That statement, just like your idea of your "self" and just like any uncomfortable physical response (emotions) you may feel when you hear it, is just another object in awareness. And when you don't take it personally, you're not threatened. That means you can be genuinely interested in what's really troubling your partner. Instead of getting caught in painful reactions, you can share warmth and support.

These simple shifts in understanding can help not only couples working to improve communication in relationships, but anyone seeking to understand—and be understood—by another person.

If you'd like to learn more about how these perspectives can help you avoid painful mistakes and have better communication with your partner, check out my Relationship Survival Kit audios in the Finding True Magic online shop at shop.findingtruemagic.com.

4

Mindfulness, Meditation, and Real Happiness

8 Ways to Develop Mindfulness and Awareness, Plus One Imagination Game

....

DEVELOPING MINDFULNESS AND AWARENESS can be like riding white-water rapids. It's easy to talk about, but actually doing it requires inner strength, stamina, and a firm resolve.

If you want to develop this inner strength and stamina, you have to take every opportunity to practice it, and little by little it gets easier!

So, I'm going to tell you 8 of my favorite ways to develop mindfulness and awareness—the basis of all forms of inner strength.

You'll soon notice that opportunities to practice are continually presenting themselves! When they do, you can practice "breaking state." This means you stop right in the middle of a habitual thought or behavior—say, for example, you're starting to worry again—and consciously act with mindfulness. Act independently of the urges of that habitual pattern.

So, I'm going to tell you about 8 interesting ways you can "break state" and practice mindfulness. (After that, I'll give you an imagination game that I think you'll enjoy.)

1. **Reverse the trend. Go slowly when you want to go fast, and vice versa.** When you feel like contracting in fear... expand! For example, if you are sliding into a poverty mentality, give something away. If someone is rude, respond with kindness. Patience is a form of generosity; cultivate patience toward

yourself and others. Give yourself both space and time: Take a deep breath and shift your perspective, look at the sky, feel your feet on the ground. Affirm that there is plenty of time to do everything, and relax the contraction. Become attentive to these habitual patterns and vary them until you feel the friction of change.

2. **Do ordinary tasks with wakeful attention.** Brush your teeth or your hair as if you were doing it for the very first time (with a beginner's mind)… or for the very last time (with awareness of the imminence of death). Notice what it's like to do these things mindfully rather than absent-mindedly and mechanically.

3. **Notice when you are basing your choices or your behaviors on external standards** (which you may have internalized) such as praise or blame, good or bad, right or wrong. Think deeply about what it means to "cause harm." Are critiques like these harmful to yourself and others in any way? Relax any concern about how you look to others. Relax any concern about how others appear to you.

4. **Take risks and perform small acts of courage.** Appreciate the courage it takes to change. Make unusual choices and plans, and then follow through. Think of something that makes you say, "That's just not me." Then try that thing you wouldn't usually do. Just do it!

5. **Practice witnessing thoughts and feelings.** Sit quietly upright and relaxed, and simply label your thoughts and feelings this way: "thinking…thinking…feeling…" Label and witness these thoughts and feelings without getting involved in them or following them. Practice until you can spend 20 minutes or more a day with this simple exercise.

6. **Cultivate mindfulness in all your actions throughout the day.** Create your own reminders or exercises for "breaking state," for waking yourself up. This is a discipline, and true discipline is an act of courage—the courage to step outside the trance of narrow self-involvement and fear. To keep it real and fresh requires that you be vigilant. If this practice becomes just a routine habit, then you've fallen asleep again. Stand tall and renew your enthusiasm! If it becomes a duty or an obligation that involves hope, fear, guilt, or an idea of gaining something, you'll become resentful about it. Remember that the right relationship to wakeful living is the goal here—not simply trading one trance for another.

7. **Become aware of how and when you are ruled by your *unexamined* likes and dislikes.** What are they? Make a list with 2 columns: Things I Like, Things I Don't Like. Begin to notice when you're reacting with revulsion or attraction to something. Ask yourself, Why do I dislike this? Or Why do I like this? What is the story you're telling yourself that makes it pleasant or unpleasant? Is there a different way you could look at it? Is there a different way you might respond to it? Practice this with experiences you like, as well as the ones you don't.

8. **Be ready to be surprised!** As you clarify and step out of your shame-based and fear-based trances, you'll be able to trust the goodness of your true self. You may be amazed at how wonderful it feels to speak and behave with mindfulness, clarity, and precision. This wonderful feeling is the direct result of your practice of mindfulness and awareness.

Now … here is an imagination game.

This game could be called a visualization, but it's really more like an intentional daydream. Imagine that your most important goal in life is a living symbol. It could be an animal, a bird, or other vivid image that has meaning for you. Relate to it, feel its energy. Take a few moments to become fully established in your relationship to your symbol so that it becomes alive for you.

Now visualize the symbol moving on a path straight out into the distance … and then up to the top of a hill.

As you make your way up the path, continue to experience the power and vividness of your chosen symbol. Walking this path symbolizes you traveling along your life path to attain your goal.

As you begin walking, you start to notice temptations and obstacles in various forms on either side of the path: people, objects of desire or fear, situations from the past, and symbols of shame and fear, sadness or grief, seduction and distraction. These manifestations can try to divert you from your path, but they cannot block your path. Nor can they prevent you from going step by step, walking wakefully and intentionally. They can't stop you or distract you because you are mindful that these obstacles are scams. You maintain an undistracted, fearless awareness of your goodness and your goal.

As you keep going, step by step, knowing that you are going to stay on this path, you become more and more focused on your goal. You relax, because you realize that you can afford to take some time to experience the tempting distractions appearing to the right of you and the left of you. You can hear and feel the pull of their old familiar scams. As you see them, it's as if their words appear in midair, like speech balloons in a comic strip: "Hurry up!" "This is dumb!" "Wouldn't a cookie taste great right now?" You happily "pop" these balloons and move on.

After taking the time you need to walk this path in a way that builds your inner strength, you arrive at the base of the hill, having left all of those obstacles and distractions behind. Take one last look back at them and notice how good it feels to have overcome them. Then turn and proceed up the hill ... into the presence of your living symbol.

You see that now your symbol has become even more vivid, meaningful, and powerful as a result of your efforts. Feel its energy permeate you as it merges fully into you, dissolving into every cell of your body, carrying its resources, intelligence, and power into every part of your being.

Take some time to experience this, knowing and sensing that it is transforming your relationships to your past and future in ways that thoroughly free you from fear and confusion. When you come back to ordinary awareness, feel yourself relating to all of your ordinary routines with a new energy of appreciation and joy.

10 Wrong Ideas
That Can Ruin
Your Mindfulness Practice

....

It seems like everybody is practicing mindfulness these days. Mindfulness has really taken off! It's showing up in corporate boardrooms, college classrooms, hospice care, and locker rooms. This is a wonderful development because, *when practiced correctly*, mindfulness holds tremendous benefits for us as individuals; for our family, friends, and coworkers; and for our communities and the world at large.

There is some confusion, though, as to what mindfulness practice actually *is*. I have heard people describe it as everything from a quick way to get rid of stress at work to a method for getting to sleep at night to attaining enlightenment or spiritual awakening.

I have also met many people who began a mindfulness practice to alleviate their anxiety in meetings or when taking tests but then quickly gave up, because they felt their mindfulness was actually making their minds wilder and more stressed-out, instead of calmer. Something was off!

Usually, instructions for beginning a mindfulness practice are pretty simple—just pay attention to your breath or your sensory experience in the moment. So what happens to mess that up? Well, sometimes new practitioners don't realize they are bringing certain wrong ideas into their mindfulness practice. These wrong ideas can completely defeat the purpose of your practice.

So…here's what not to think when you're practicing mindfulness:

1. **"This isn't calming me down! My mind is getting even wilder!"**
When you begin practicing mindfulness, you start to see what's going on in your mind. You become aware of just how wild your habitual thought patterns really are. Don't stop at this point! Don't be tricked and think, "I don't know how to control this wildness, this is terrible!" Instead, just keep putting your energy into being aware of this mental activity. The more energy you put into watching your mind, the less energy is available for your mind to go wild. As you just watch your mind's activity, moment by moment, it will begin to get quieter.

2. **"Mindfulness is an emergency relaxation technique for when I feel like I'm losing it."**
It's certainly true that mindfulness is a useful technique for calming yourself down and decompressing. But that's not all it is. Mindfulness may give you the relief you seek, but if you only practice it when you have an acute need—like when your heart is pounding after your boss has just yelled at you—the benefits of your mindfulness practice will be very short-term.

    To get the most from your mindfulness practice, think of it as a demonstration of your interest in getting to know yourself deeply and thoroughly, not as a quick fix.

3. **"Mindfulness practice requires time I just don't have."**
You could be thinking, "If I have to spend a lot of time doing mindfulness practice, it's not for me." But consider this: If you find yourself in intolerable circumstances or relationships fairly often, maybe it would be useful to come to know more about the way your mind works. Wouldn't it be helpful to know exactly how you end up making choices that tend

to create stress and suffering? That's what mindfulness is, and it really just means getting to know yourself better. And, like getting to know anyone or anything, it requires paying attention little by little, over time. Only then can you gain insight and understanding from your self-observations.

4. **"This is boring. I need something with more juice!"**
Committing to practice mindfulness, even for a few minutes each day, demonstrates your desire to know yourself better and understand your choices more completely. If you remind yourself, "This is my time to spend with myself," it will make your daily mindfulness practice easy and enjoyable. Instead of dreading another "boring practice session," you can feel a joyful anticipation to spend time with your best friend.

With daily mindfulness practice, you will quite naturally develop kindness, appreciation, patience, and self-encouragement as you see more and more clearly what your habitual thought patterns are and how they have been causing you problems. As you see and release these habitual patterns over time, all sense of boredom or ingratitude will leave you. What could be more interesting than watching that happen in yourself?!

5. **"I'm going to become a really mindful person."**
Once we have decided to practice mindfulness, we may rely on our typical way of thinking, which means focusing on this new skill until we become "good" at it. So, what's wrong with that? Nothing … if you're learning to drive or cook spaghetti. But mindfulness practice is a little different—in it, we let go of expecting a certain outcome.

Most of us have a habit of looking for a quick payoff from what we do. The faster we can get our to-do list done, the better. We push. We hurry. It seems to make perfect sense that the faster we go, the quicker we will get there. We want results, now! But, becoming mindful—gaining self-knowledge—is not accomplished by following this logic. To gain self-knowledge, the opposite is true: The slower you go, the faster you will get there.

6. **"I'm going to focus on mindfulness 110 percent!"**
As the story goes (and I'm paraphrasing here), a musician once asked the Buddha how to practice mindfulness. The Buddha asked the musician, "When you prepare to play your lyre, do you tighten the strings to the point of breaking, or do you let them sag loosely?" The musician replied, "Neither, Sir. I make sure they are not too tight or too loose." The Buddha said, "In the same way, when you practice mindfulness, do not be too tight or too loose in your effort. Find the balance that keeps your mind fresh and alert."

It's great to have an attitude of resolve when you begin your mindfulness practice, but don't overdo your effort. Overdoing it creates more agitated activity in your mind, which makes it harder for you to simply observe your mind's natural state.

7. **"If I practice mindfulness, I'll become worthy."**
We feel unworthy when we're out of touch with ourselves. Almost everyone has an intuitive sense, a gut feeling that can always be trusted. If we lose trust in our own natural intuitive sense, we reject this guidance and start fearfully second-guessing. We place more importance on what others may think of our choices than on our own intuitive sense of what's right. Decisions become difficult to make, and we eventually lose our sensitivity to our intuitive sense of the right thing to do. By practicing mindfulness, we regain this essential connection to our intuition. We recognize that we

don't become worthy by practicing mindfulness. Instead, we discover that our self-worth was, is, and always will be indisputable. Mindfulness gives us the clarity to see this.

8. **"I have to go on a retreat, or at least on vacation, to practice mindfulness."**
We may think we have to go off to some quiet, solitary place in order to do mindfulness practice. The fact is, mindfulness can be practiced anytime, on the spot. You can watch your mind, your choices, and your actions at any point during your day and learn something about yourself.

Practicing mindfulness gradually frees you from habitual thoughts of hope and fear, success and failure. Once we no longer fear failure or are driven to succeed, we can be quite content practicing mindfulness moment by moment, anywhere at all. We develop an attitude of equanimity. My wife's dear great-aunt had such equanimity. When something painful or challenging happened, she would say, quite cheerfully, "That's all just part of it!"

9. **"If I just pay really close attention to chopping these vegetables, I'm practicing mindfulness."**
There isn't anything wrong with focusing on the present moment, appreciating the color of the veggies you're chopping, and taking great care with the chef's knife you're using to do it. This brings you pleasure as you work in the kitchen and greatly decreases your odds of cutting yourself. But it's important to be aware of what's going on all around you as well. My teacher Dzogchen Ponlop Rinpoche calls this "360-degree mindfulness." If a fire breaks out in the living room and we remain completely focused on cutting the brilliant green zucchini into beautiful, uniform slices, how far does that kind of mindfulness take us? Our mindfulness can

begin with a focus on our breath and our sensory perceptions, as well as awareness of our inner world of thoughts
and feelings, but it also needs to include our surroundings—
above, below, and on all sides.

10. **"I'm a lot more mindful than most people I know."**
Even if you get off on the right foot and practice mindfulness
very diligently, it is important to be alert to the tendency to
judge and compare. Watch to see if you're keeping track of
your progress in relation to how you think others are doing,
assigning gold stars and black marks in the little notebook in
your mind.

In mindfulness practice, you are practicing developing sensitivity
to your natural intelligent awareness. This awareness cannot be
improved upon. It is complete as it is, and so it cannot be rightly
judged. By experiencing this completeness, you recognize your
natural state of worthiness. When you have this experience, you
discover an effortless capacity to care about others. Comparing
yourself to them no longer crosses your mind.

As you discard these wrong ideas, your mindfulness practice
will become one of the great, joyful activities of your life.

Good luck!

You Can
Meditate

....

PEOPLE OFTEN TELL ME, "I know I should meditate. But I've tried and I just can't do it."

Does that sound familiar?

Information about meditation is all over the place. And there is so much conflicting advice about meditation that it is very common for people to get confused about what meditation is and how to do it.

WHAT IS MEDITATION?

A common misconception is that "doing meditation right" means having a calm and quiet mind.

But ironically, when a person first begins to meditate, they experience their mind racing with even more thoughts. Actually, we aren't having more thoughts. But simply because now we're sitting still, we start noticing the vast quantity of thoughts we always have!

Not realizing this, new meditators easily get discouraged and may quit right away, thinking, "There's no point in meditating. It just makes things worse!"

If we were lucky enough to be taught to *expect* that we'll have lots of thoughts when we meditate—and if we keep meditating— the next trap is thinking that we should be "getting somewhere."

Day after day in our meditation, we see thoughts and still more thoughts. We may think, "Okay, I have patiently followed the instructions to be still. I understand I am noticing my thoughts the way they have always been. I get it that my thoughts are not getting worse just because I am meditating. But…nothing else is happening. Shouldn't something be getting better?"

The mistake here is in thinking that meditation is supposed to produce something—a product or a payoff. Of course, some people meditate only to relax or become more productive at work, and those can definitely become by-products of a person meditating. But that certainly is not all that meditation does…and it is not what meditation is for.

Meditation doesn't create something new and separate from you. It only "works," so to speak, if you let go of the idea of a payoff or achievement.

Think of it this way: If you spent 5 minutes a day looking at yourself in the mirror, would you expect that effort to produce some new "thing"—some payoff that would appear on the counter at the side of the sink? Of course not. What would happen is that you'd become more familiar with the details of your own face—nothing more.

Real meditation is like this. Instead of looking at your face in the mirror, you're looking at your mind. As you meditate regularly, you get to notice more and more about your mind and yourself.

If you look for some payoff for meditation ("I spent this many hours, so I should have X amount of peace, love, and happiness by now"), you don't appreciate that you are just getting to know yourself. And actually, that is the best possible payoff! As you get to know yourself, you become aware of what you truly care about. As this awareness becomes more vivid and clear, you discover that you have the passion and courage to act on what is truly important to you, regardless of what others may think. Then life becomes more and more satisfying. As Aristotle said, "Knowing yourself is the beginning of all wisdom."

Even though wisdom is naturally present in everyone, to meet a truly wise person is rare in this world. For anyone who wants to uncover that wisdom, meditation is essential. When you cultivate the courage to get to know yourself and your mind, wisdom gradually begins to shine forth.

HOW TO MEDITATE

Here are 4 things that will help you meditate for real:

1. **Be interested in the fact that you are alive.** This may sound odd, but it's key. In many ways, we have been trained to be numb to being alive. For now, just sit quietly and breathe. Be interested in feeling what it's like to be alive. Let this feeling become more and more vivid. Notice all you can about how this feels.

2. **Ask questions and challenge your thoughts.** Let's say that you have the thought, "I should have a quiet, calm mind right now." But you're agitated and struggling because clearly you don't have a quiet, calm mind. Stop struggling and ask, "Who says so?" Notice what happens when you ask this question with interest.

3. **Don't fight with anything that comes into your awareness.** Just look at it and then let it go.

4. **Let go of your habit of knowing what things are.** Instead, *ask* what they are, and then relax and look without expecting an immediate answer. Be like a 4-year-old looking at fish in a pond. Just look … and let yourself enjoy whatever you discover.

The essence of meditation is to be freshly interested in your mind and your life, just as it is, moment by moment, without judgment. Enjoy your meditation. Enjoy yourself!

Simple
Meditation
Instructions

....

Now that you know what to do and what to avoid when you're meditating, here are some simple meditation instructions you can use anytime you like.

1. **Begin by doing some easy stretches:** your arms, legs, and neck. Then take a few deep breaths, pushing out gently on the exhale to empty your lungs. Let the inhale come naturally.

2. **Set a time limit**—in the beginning, your meditation session can be just 5 or 10 minutes. Make it a short and easy enough period of time that you won't talk yourself out of doing it! As you adapt to this nurturing activity, you will enjoy extending the time period.

3. **Sit in a comfortable upright position** with your spine straight but not tense—naturally upright. You can sit on a cushion or chair—whichever you find is best for remaining relaxed, still, upright, and alert. Place your hands on your thighs or your knees.

4. **Feel your breathing.** Let it be natural. When you notice your mind has wandered off, come back to focusing on your felt sense of breathing. No judgment—just come back.

5. **Let awareness and perceptions flow**—don't try to block or hold on to anything. Cultivate a refreshed interest, moment by moment.

That's it! You are now getting to know the flow of your mind and body aliveness as it manifests from moment to moment.

What If I
Don't Have Time
for Meditation?

....

THE BENEFITS OF A regular meditation practice are now widely recognized, thanks to pioneering studies by Harvard researchers and others. Even so, people often ask, "But what if I don't have *time* to meditate?" This is such a common concern that it really deserves to be resolved.

If we take this question on its own terms, then quite literally we are accepting that there is no possible solution. There is simply no time to meditate!

But what if we challenge the presupposition here? If we don't automatically accept that there is "no time" or "not enough time" to meditate, then we can easily recognize that the situation isn't hopeless. Consider these perspectives:

- **Whether we have "enough time" for anything is a function of how we choose to spend our time.** Every day we make choices about what to spend our time doing and what we will not spend time doing.

- **If we're not meditating, then clearly we simply are not valuing the choice to spend time meditating over and above other activities.** Let's meditate on this for a moment.

I "SHOULD" BE MEDITATING

Are you being influenced by "shoulds" and "have tos"? Do you think you should meditate to please someone else and not yourself? Without a genuine interest, you won't get very far.

In popular culture, mindfulness and meditation are trending while social media is fanning public interest in practicing these mind training exercises. Is your motivation for meditating only to join the crowd?

Or, have you tried meditation and decided you can't do it? I often hear people say, "I couldn't stop thinking—in fact, my wild thinking seemed to get even worse while I was meditating!" If so, it's important to consider several things.

Like many people, you may have learned a mistaken or incomplete notion of what meditation is. First, meditation is not about stopping yourself from thinking, or attaining some special experience that proves you are okay or even "saved." People new to meditation practice often believe that it is making them have more thoughts. In reality, being quiet and still—and paying attention to your body, breath, and mind—simply make you more aware of how many thoughts you've been having all along! The fact that you have a multitude of thoughts is nothing new. What's new is that, when you meditate, you notice these thoughts flowing through your mind.

THE MYTH OF "GOOD MEDITATION"

Most meditators have thought many times during a single session, "Am I doing it right?" But there is no "right" experience of meditation. Naturally, we want to "succeed" at being a "good meditator." But real meditation is just "meeting" yourself ("hello" with a smile) and being with yourself just as you are, moment by moment.

Real meditation is practice, not perfection. It's about staying with a felt sense of yourself instead of going off into distracted thinking and daydreams. And when you notice you have strayed, simply come back—no worries! Just come back to yourself in a friendly way ... and renew your interest in the experience of breathing and being alive, moment by moment.

There is no such thing as an objectively good or bad meditation. You might enjoy some sessions more than others, but no meditation is better than another.

MEDITATION IS TAKING TIME FOR A MIRACLE

It is truly a miracle that you exist at all. What are the odds? Meditation is simply taking time to be interested in this fact—not as an intellectual speculation, but as a growing felt-sense awareness of literally being birthed by life.

Isn't it amazing? Moment by moment, breath by breath, heartbeat by heartbeat ... it's all a gift! Meditation is getting interested in how you relate to the miracle that you exist.

As you meditate, you begin to appreciate more and more that this miraculous gift of life and conscious intelligence forms the basis of everything else in your life as well. You naturally become more interested in gaining a stronger and stronger appreciation of this gift of life. And you also grow less and less interested in being distracted by—and wasting time on—superficial thoughts.

What kind of thought is a superficial time-waster? Any thought that prevents you from experiencing the sweetness of contacting your aliveness, simply and directly.

The more that you meditate, you'll start to notice that this simple contact with yourself makes you feel better emotionally, clearer mentally, and more energized physically. Then you can easily choose to make time to meditate because you'll want to continue unfolding your experience of the benefits of being with yourself.

3 WAYS TO MAKE TIME FOR MEDITATION

Of course, we're not really talking about "making time." That's a little silly. Time is a mental construct, so essentially we can "make" as much of it as we want! But here are some ways you can make time to meditate. They will help you choose your own good times for meditation.

1. **Meditate for a few moments when you first wake up and just before you go to bed.** These are great times to meditate because they tend to be gaps when you are more relaxed and not fully engaged in speedy, distracted mind states.

2. **Stop often during the day, for 30 seconds or so, to relax as best you can and breathe and feel your body.** This counts as meditation! Try doing this on the hour every hour—it will change your whole experience of your day.

3. **Pick a regular special place in your home for daily meditation.** You can start with short sessions, maybe 10 or 20 minutes, and build up from there as your body and mind become familiar with meditation practice.

It is easy to make time to meditate. All you have to do is give up a little of the time and energy you usually put into creating distractions, worries, and drama in your life! Relax, breathe, and consider the miracle that you exist, that everything exists along with you, and that all of this is taking place in endless variety and with such brilliant qualities. Enjoy!

Is Your Problem
Time Management
or FOMO?

....

MANY PEOPLE PROCRASTINATE (and freeze) themselves when they have to make an important decision or organize a project. They think, "I'm terrible at this! I can't seem to decide what to do, or when to do it." But very often the problem is actually FOMO—the fear of missing out.

Hundreds of clients have told us just that—they're afraid of committing to or deciding on one thing because then they might miss out on something better.

This logic is puzzling for 3 important reasons:

1. If you procrastinate and freeze yourself, you are *already* missing out on those imaginary "better things" you think will slip away if you commit to "this thing" you're considering. But in addition to that, you're missing out on "this thing"! That is what happens when you freeze yourself. You don't get to enjoy either option.

2. We freeze ourselves this way due to faulty logic. We mistakenly think, "If I commit to something, I'll miss out on something better. But if all I do is procrastinate, I won't miss out on anything!" And yet we're totally missing out, because we're frozen in procrastination!

3. Of course, if we take action and make the choice—any choice—we will certainly miss out on this state of frozenness and procrastination!

It is true that you can miss out on good or better things when you make any choice. As soon as we make a choice, we exclude the other options that depend on that choice. If I choose to go to the Fred Meyer store for my groceries, I miss out on all the things and people I might have encountered at Whole Foods, Safeway, and so on. With any choice you make, you could make a long list of possibilities you're missing out on as a result of your decision.

Missing out is unavoidable. But you can absolutely avoid the fear of missing out.

Even people with FOMO do make some choices. For some odd reason, FOMO seems to kick in only when we are presented with a choice we believe is very important.

In the case of a "very important choice," we build up the expectation that the choice we decline to make has a high and unique value. Along with this expectation comes the fear that missing out on it will create pain and suffering.

Of course, that is not the case with choices like my Fred Meyer grocery store example. I'm not anxious thinking that Whole Foods or Safeway has something better than I can get at Fred Meyer. If I find out that they do have something better, I'll go there next time. But I'm not stressed out about it.

When we experience FOMO, we're in the grip of a fear that tells us, "You're missing out on an irreplaceable opportunity—a very important one that may never come again." For example: "If I commit to a relationship with this person, I might miss out on meeting someone even better—my soulmate." If you miss out on this one, you've missed out forever! It's clearly not the same as being able to go to Safeway for your groceries the next time.

When you choose one romantic partner, you will probably never know if there was a "better" romantic partner available for you. But if you get stuck in FOMO always looking for greener pastures, you'll probably make yourself and your partner miserable in the process.

THE 5 INSIGHTS YOU NEED TO FREE YOURSELF FROM FOMO

1. **When we have FOMO, we have fallen for the idea that external objects have a magical quality that will make us complete and happy.** But of course, nothing has value until we *give* it value. You may want to own a steel-blue Land Rover more than anything, but we could easily find 10 people who couldn't care less about owning that vehicle. If the Rover had the inherent power to make itself wanted, then everyone would have to want it. But, it doesn't have that power, does it? Neither objects nor events have any inherent power to make us want them.

2. **We give value to everything we desire simply by telling ourselves it is valuable.** "This is the best one. I need it, I want it, I have to have it." When we repeat such thoughts to ourselves, we are literally giving ourselves *hypnotic suggestions*. The objects of our desire are rarely required by the laws of nature. If they are truly required, they are needs, not mere desires. But our desire can masquerade as need…when we accept the suggestion that we must have the object we desire.

3. **Since the desire is a hypnotic suggestion we are giving ourselves, it is imaginary, not real.** How do we fall for this illusion? Simple! We restrict our breathing and create tension in various areas of our body, which creates fear and stress. Then we whisper to ourselves another suggestion: "You can't breathe normally or relax until you get…this!"

4. **Since FOMO lies in your imagination, you can get free of it by deciding to imagine in a different way.** Instead of suggesting to yourself that you will be empty and bereft if you miss out, suggest to yourself that it's okay to keep breathing properly and to let your body be completely at ease…even if you do miss out! Breathing properly and remaining fully at ease gives your body the permission to generate wonderful feelings such as peace, joy, and enthusiasm.

    The body-mind experience of these feeling qualities results in a state of happiness—that's what we really desire anyway. But somehow we learned over time that, unless we obtained the outer "whatever-it-is," we would not be able to feel happy and complete.

5. **Here's how you can imagine differently and get free of FOMO.** Say to yourself,

    - "Even though I may not satisfy my desire and even though I may miss out on something, I breathe easily and relax."

    - I choose to think about things that make me feel happy and complete. I am grateful to be alive."

    - "I love myself more and more day by day, and I feel confident making that effort regardless of the outcome."

    - "I deal with everything with a relaxed, happy state of mind that grows brighter day by day."

You can create a long list of such encouraging suggestions to replace the negative ones. In fact, when you practice affirming these encouraging suggestions, it causes your subconscious mind to create new ones and deliver those to you, too!

Practice makes perfect. The more you practice thinking this way, the more quickly and easily you will generate wonderful states of completion and wholeness.

Remember, you give importance to outer objects or accomplishments by choosing to give them value through the power of your imagination and hypnotic suggestion.

IMAGINING "AS IF"

You can also practice simply imagining that you already have the objects of your desire. You can imagine this so vividly that you actually create the feeling state that you think comes from having them.

Ask, "How would I feel if I had this just the way I want it?" and vividly imagine it being so…and feel the feelings that having it gives you. Then notice that you're truly feeling the feelings you want to have simply by the right use of your imagination … and then drop the unnecessary object desire.

With practice, you will naturally recognize more and more clearly that you don't need to chase outer desires to feel fantastic. You learn to generate inner happy states directly by properly using your own power of imagination. You also recognize that generating the fear of missing out was, is, and always will be your own mind game.

This realization is freeing and fun! You realize the FOMO was a big deal only because you were playing an imaginary trick on yourself. The basic debilitating suggestion is, "I must have that. It is the only thing that will make me happy." But the hidden debilitating suggestion is, "If I miss out, I will never be able to breathe easily or relax my body and mind to create wonderful feelings." And you know that's just silly.

By continuing to practice this simple exercise, you will easily prove that these suggestions are arbitrary and untrue flimsy opinions. You'll regain your ability to generate free, relaxed, happy-to-be-alive states, even when your desires are not met. Go for it!

5

Worry and Self-Doubt, Kindness and Confidence

Feeling
Helpless?

....

AT THIS TIME, THE COVID-19 pandemic has taken our notion of the world's suffering in a whole new direction, one that now includes us all in a very intimate way. Many people are experiencing fear and grave concern about the future. More than ever, it is important to strengthen our spirit and clarity of mind to deal with the challenges we are likely to face in our world.

During a recent interview, someone said to me, "I feel helpless in the face of the world's suffering. I don't know what to do about the pain I see all around me. It's driving me crazy."

My response was basically this: "You know, it takes a lot of energy and attention to drive yourself crazy." If you redirect that energy away from "feeling helpless" and bring it into alignment with your desire to benefit, you may come up with some creative solutions. I'll explain.

"I feel helpless" is actually a judgment, not a feeling. But when we label judgments as feelings, we trap ourselves. Why? Because then we respond to the judgment as though it is a feeling, as though it is a part of us.

If you think you're helpless, if you believe the thought that you're helpless, you're going to feel sad and discouraged. Anybody would. That just shows that you work perfectly well; it doesn't mean the judgment is part of your being.

You see, the thing is, our feelings are simply our own being, vibrating. Just as there is a certain vibratory level that our organ of sight (our eye) can perceive as sight, and just as there is a type of vibratory level that our ears can hear, in the same way, we experience a different band of vibration as emotions. And that's just us, vibrating.

In the hypnotic nature of our mind—take nouns, for example—we label emotions such as joy, sadness, anger, or whatever. And because we give them these labels, we think they're separate things. So, we may say, "I have a problem with *anger*, I'm going to solve my *anger* problem, I'm going to get rid of it." And so we repress the anger. As we go along day to day, after a while we notice, "Well, I'm not angry anymore...but I'm not that joyful, either."

Why is that? It's because we can't single out one emotion and repress it. That emotion is our very capacity to vibrate, in action. In order to repress an emotion—any emotion—we have to freeze our whole capacity to vibrate. That's the only way you can reduce an emotional response.

So, that's the first thing. Our emotions are a manifestation of us vibrating in a certain way. They are our very being, vibrating. That's why we have absolute conviction in the truth of the emotion— because that emotion is our very being, vibrating with life.

In this case, the vibration is sadness and discouragement, because you believe the thought, "I'm helpless." But if you say "I feel helpless," you're transferring the truth of life vibrating to that thought of helplessness. Then we're convinced, because we think, "Am I helpless? Yeah, I can feel it right here in my chest."

But no. The true thought is, "When I believe I am helpless...I feel sad and discouraged." Do I have to believe I'm helpless? Well, maybe I do, maybe I am! At that point, you could take a moment to think about it. You don't have to try to fight with it and come to some quick decision.

You can say to yourself, "Okay, I'll be open-minded. I may be helpless, but it's only fair that you give me the evidence. If you give me the evidence that I'm helpless, then I'll believe it. But until you can give me the evidence, I'm not going to feel sad and discouraged. And I'm not going to drive myself crazy."

HERE'S HOW TO HELP YOURSELF OUT OF HELPLESSNESS

First, try this for a moment: Examine a familiar negative feeling. Something like, "I feel like I'll never succeed" or "I feel like I'm not good enough" or "I feel like she is prettier than me."

Now notice the language of these bad feelings. They each contain "feel like." Almost any time someone says "I feel like," what comes after "like" will be a judgment, not a feeling. During the normal course of your day, catch these "feel like" thoughts, and you'll develop your ability to recognize that whatever comes after "feel like" is a judgment, not a feeling.

Once you have some clarity about your "feel like" thoughts, practice restructuring them: "When I believe the judgment _____ (fill in the blank), what do I feel?" Listen within for a moment. Then ask, "What is the evidence that is convincing me to believe this judgment?" Notice what you discover.

You can write or sketch this exercise in a journal so that you can keep track of and study what comes up.

Two important tips: A feeling statement will contain an emotion: "I feel sad" or "I feel angry." Also, make sure you don't answer the "What do I feel?" question with another judgment, such as "I feel like a weirdo." If you notice you're doing this, simply restructure this statement too: "When I believe X and Y, what do I feel? Is there any valid evidence?" Valid means accurate, according to the laws of cause and effect, not according to the opinion of others. "That's what my father always told me" doesn't count as valid evidence!

This process may seem surprisingly challenging at first, because we are so habituated to labeling judgments as feelings. But keep at it. Enjoy your mind at work! You can teach it to work with wonderful clarity for your own benefit … and be free of helpless feelings forever!

How to Stop Worrying
and Enjoy Making Plans

....

NOT LONG AGO SOMEONE asked me, "Isn't making plans just another way of worrying?"

We might ask this question out of a belief that planning ahead indicates a lack of spontaneity—that it's better to just "go with the flow" and let life unfold as it will. Of course, a plan isn't a prison. While following our plan, we can still leave room to be spontaneous and enjoy being surprised!

More often, though, as soon as we start making plans, we habitually start getting worried. But why do we make plans? So that we can accomplish something! Nothing is wrong with that, so why are we worrying? The worry is *really* about whether our plans will succeed or fail.

It seems so natural, doesn't it? How many times have we heard someone say, "Of course I worry … because I care."

Yes, we worry and yes, we care, but there is not an automatic link between the two. Yet, over the years I've heard many people insist, with agonizing passion, that they just can't let go of worry. How can you expect a parent to stop worrying about a child who may be in danger? Or about any potential loss? Worrying seems tied to caring. Worry seems so natural.

The key word here is "seems." States of mind and thought patterns such as worry seem natural only because of repetition and familiarity. We believe them, not because they're true, but simply because we have thought about them over and over again. All this ruminating can become a strong habit.

Once we get habituated to one way of thinking or ruminating, a weird thing happens. Instead of seeing our state of mind or thought pattern as merely one point of view among many other possible points of view, we begin to believe it is the truth. It's a poor way to decide on the truth, to be sure, but unless we keep watch over it with mindfulness, that's how our minds tend to work.

When my clients express a conviction that they can't let go of worry (for example, because that worry is about their child), it is usually possible to help them stop worrying in about 10 minutes.

HOW TO STOP WORRYING IN 10 MINUTES OR LESS

These 5 reminders will usually help you nip your worries in the bud:

1. Caring doesn't require that you worry. Honor your caring heart.

2. Refusing to engage in worry doesn't mean you don't care.

3. Worrying is an activity like any activity. All activities produce results.

4. Instead of just getting swept up in worrying thoughts, look at the results of worrying. Does it create any helpful results? And have you noticed that worry is infectious? The primary result of worrying is that the worry intensifies and you get others to worry, too!

5. When you need to focus on a problem or care about someone, worry is unnecessary. You literally do not need to worry. You can simply focus, with care.

Even after reading these reminders, you still may feel attached to worrying. Why? Because we usually need a new and better option to hold onto before we can really let go of our current attachment.

HERE'S A BETTER OPTION THAN WORRYING

First, let's look at the structure of worry—how it works:

1. **Worry starts with a *motivation*, an *interest*, something you care about.** So, you could say it starts with love. When you're interested in something, you are giving it value. That interest itself is a kind and loving gesture.

2. **As soon as you develop such a motivation or interest, you start projecting a *desired future outcome*.** This outcome is also infused with your love, and that love in turn is expressed in the way you give value to that outcome.

   Getting from Point A (your motivation) to Point B (your desired future outcome) requires action. Whether or not you reach that outcome is determined by what kind of action you take. Unfortunately, merely having a worthy motivation and a worthy goal doesn't guarantee that you'll make correct, worthy choices of action.

   Maybe you've heard the phrase "The road to hell is paved with good intentions." When you worry, your actions are fearful, repetitive imaginings. Again and again you project mental images of your desired goals not working out. Worry generates and radiates disturbing, fear-inducing energy. And for as long as your thinking is clouded by fear, you'll continue to make poor choices.

3. **But consider this: *Prayer,* or a *heartfelt aspiration*, has the same structure as worry...with one *very important difference*.** In the prayer scenario, Point A (your motivation) and Point B (your desired outcome) remain the same, but wait...Point C is very different. When you pray or make an aspiration—no belief in a god required—you are engaged in repetitive, loving thinking. Loving thinking generates and radiates encouraging

energy. So, in a state of prayer or aspiration, you just naturally make better choices. Why? Because your mind is clear and your heart is open. In this state, solutions of a much higher quality spontaneously begin to enter your awareness.

WORRY IS NEGATIVE PRAYER

What does all this mean? It means that worry is negative prayer. Now that you see this clearly, try this: Put your hands out in front of you, palms up. Imagine filling one of your hands with worries and filling the other hand with prayers. Reflect on the consequences of each activity. Which would you rather give your energy to? Worry or prayer? So far, everyone I know who has tried this has said "prayer"!

Worry is negative prayer that produces negative outcomes. As you shift from a state of worry and choose to pray or make a heartfelt aspiration instead, you are entering a resourceful, prayerful state that instantly increases your chances for a beneficial outcome. Once you recognize the better choice, it's easy to practice making this change.

One last thing—the shift from worry to prayer is not a one-shot deal. The habit of worrying won't disappear overnight; it will probably keep coming into your mind for a while. But that habit's not a problem anymore because now you understand its nature. And now you recognize that you have a better choice. In fact, you can now begin using the appearance of worry as a reminder. When the "worry bell" rings, it's your reminder to pray about whatever is the focus of that worry. Again, no belief in a god is required here, only a willingness to pray. And by substituting worry with prayer, you're inviting better outcomes.

How to
Invite Success

....

SOMETIMES PEOPLE, ESPECIALLY YOUNG people considering their future, will say, "But what if I don't succeed? What if I fail?" Hearing this often sends me into a personal reverie.

When I was 20 years old, I dropped out of college to enter a Buddhist monastery. This was in 1967 when this was still considered a very unusual thing to do. My family was horrified and mystified. My college friends were concerned to see me abandoning the success that they believed an Ivy League education would ensure.

I didn't care. I was passionate about following through on my sudden inspiration to set out on this adventure, even though everyone around me thought it was extremely foolhardy.

As time passed and I settled into meditation practice at the Zen Center in San Francisco, which owned and operated the Tassajara Monastery, I came back to earth a bit. I was going to have to figure out how to make a living. But now, as a college dropout, I had no clear idea how to do it. Out walking in the city one day near a busy intersection, I just stopped and sat down on a fire hydrant! Looking off into the distance, I felt aimless, terrified by my unknown future.

Many years later, I realized that the terror I felt then actually had little to do with the unknown. It was more about the "known" lurking behind what then appeared as an "unknown."

Outside my conscious awareness was a subtle "known"—a belief that I was obligated to live up to my parents' expectations.

At that time, I deeply believed, even though I wasn't clearly aware of it, that I was required to be a "success" in the eyes of others. This very common belief results in an equally common stressed-out state. When we're in this state, we may call it "fear of what other people think."

When this dawned on me many years later, I realized there was no hard-and-fast rule that I had to live up to my parents' expectations. With that perspective, I could have sat on that fire hydrant and had a very different experience.

Instead of being gripped by fear, I might have regarded my unknown future with eager interest. I might have felt excited and inspired to explore and discover my options and to create my life according to my true interests. No fear of making mistakes and no fear of what other people would think!

Over the years, I have often spoken with young people graduating from high school or college who feel frightened and intimidated in the face of their unknown future. When I share the insight I wish I'd had on that day in San Francisco—that there was no rule saying I had to live up to my parents' expectations—they breathe a great sigh of relief. Then they often say, "I wish someone had told me that earlier!"

Every one of us has the right—and the responsibility—to decide what success means for ourselves. Once we've done that, it is our right and privilege to go after it. We are not here to please others.

We may make a few mistakes on our path of exploration and discovery. But *mistakes are not synonymous with failure.* Mistakes are simply how we learn. Mistakes are how everyone learns, no matter our age.

So, what do you do if all this makes sense to you, but it seems impractical? How do you apply this "on the ground"? It's helpful to ask yourself some questions first. I'll suggest a few of those in a moment.

Remember, as you go, that success is not a one-time event accompanied by balloons and a dance party. Life brings us all sorts of small successes too: the fresh smell of grass after rain, the warm smile of a child or a coworker in response to our own smile, a well-deserved promotion at work, or a friend's offer of help at just the right moment.

Do these add up to success in life? What does it mean to succeed?

HERE ARE 5 QUESTIONS TO ASK YOURSELF TO HELP YOU INVITE SUCCESS

To invite success, you first need to know what it means for you. Answering these questions and then considering your answers will help you gain clarity. This clarity, or clear thinking, is the first step in opening the way to success. Okay, here are the 5 questions:

1. **What are my beliefs about success? If I imagine myself having success, what does that look like?** (And what does it feel like?)

2. **When I think about my future, what is foremost in my mind?** (Do I consider what interests me and would bring me a joyful, fulfilling life? Or do I focus on pleasing others? If the latter, who do I think I need to please? Why? Is that really true?)

3. **If I set aside what others may think, what does my heart say about ways to use my time, talents, and interests?** (There are no wrong answers. Also, your heart is allowed to change its mind.)

4. **When I think about exploring a few interesting possibilities, what springs to mind?**

5. **What are 3 simple actions I could take in the next week to begin exploring these possibilities?**

Once you have arrived at some clarity, begin exploring. You will learn more as you go along. Be open to being surprised! As you become clear about these insights and more skilled at using them, you're accomplishing the essential success in life—to be kind and encouraging to yourself and others, regardless of how projects and plans turn out. Keep your good spirit. As we said in the 1960s, thanks to the American cartoonist Robert Crumb, "Keep on truckin'."

No one owns your life except you. Go out and live it!

How Can
I Be
More Kind?

....

IF YOUR GOAL IS to be genuinely kind to others (and to be kinder to yourself), but you're having trouble doing it, clearly something is holding you back. To find out what that is, it's important to examine your *assumptions* about kindness.

Now, before we go on, let's stop and take a moment. What do you think may be holding you back? In just a moment, I'd like you to take a break and give this a few minutes. Ask, What do I think is holding me back from being kinder to myself and others? Then write down what you discover.

Press Pause now and take a few minutes to do that.

Okay. How did it go? Now I'm going to ask you to consider some more questions about kindness and go a little deeper.

START BEING KIND TO YOURSELF WITH THESE 7 QUESTIONS

Now you're going to consider these questions without self-judgment ... just asking yourself these questions to see what you can learn about your relationship with kindness. If you find you're carrying around any of these mistaken or negative ideas about kindness, see if you can challenge them a little bit.

1. Are you telling yourself you "should" want to be kind to others? Are you making kindness into a project or an obligation?

2. Do you think that, if you don't feel like being kind, it proves you're a "bad person"?

3. Are you trying to be a "good person" according to your childhood or parental programming? Does this cause you to think of kindness as a burden?

4. Do you tend to keep score? Do you want to make sure that if you extend kindness, you will be noticed? Do you want to make sure you will receive a kindness in return?

5. Are you afraid your kindness will be mocked or rejected? "Aren't you the Little Goody Two-Shoes!" "Why are you doing this? What are you getting out of it?" If we have met with such harsh responses in the past, we still may be carrying these disapproving messages around with us. Fear can prevent us from opening our hearts to be kind.

6. Are you afraid that if you're kind, people will take advantage of you? Being kind involves some degree of vulnerability. Kindness takes courage and a bit of trust.

7. Do you think you have to feel loving and kind before you can do an act of kindness? You don't! One of the most important bits of wisdom one can have is to recognize that you can choose to take action regardless of what you think or feel. Here is a simple example I often share with my clients: Many people wake up in the morning and FEEL like staying in bed. But they make the choice to get out of bed. Why? Because they place a higher value on the rewards of getting up in the morning ("I'll keep my job") than they do on enjoying the cozy feeling of sleeping in.

It is a kindness to yourself to examine any fearful, shaming ideas you may have picked up about yourself in relation to kindness. It's your mind, after all. You and only you have the power to dismiss these negative ideas that block your natural openness to connecting with others. Any one of these mistakes in our thinking can stop us from opening our hearts and being kind.

You can start with the getting-out-of-bed example I just mentioned. Think of an aspiration you have toward kindness. Make it specific—what is one simple kindness you could do today?

When you decide on one kind act—something you value more than your passing thoughts and emotions—you will easily begin to cultivate your capacity to act with kindness. It won't matter what you are thinking and feeling. You'll just do it because you've decided it matters to you. The more you practice acting on your higher principles, the easier and more natural it becomes.

Not only that, but research has shown us that being kind increases our happiness!

7 SIMPLE WAYS TO MAKE KINDNESS A HABIT

1. **Slow down physically and mentally.** Yes, slowing down is actually a high principle! When we interrupt our speedy habits of thinking and acting, we can feel the natural softness and goodness of our being. We also appreciate that others need love and care as much as we do. From within this natural softening, we become aware of our basic goodness. And then quite naturally we begin to have inspirations to act with kindness.

2. **Question and challenge your thoughts and feelings.** Don't let them fool you. Where are they really coming from? Do you have to believe fearful or mean-spirited judgments? Do you have to believe anything just because other people do?

3. **Remember, even if you get stuck on such beliefs and think you can't let them go, you can still choose to act with kindness**—even in the midst of feeling worried or tense. Do a few small acts of kindness every day. Smiling at 3 or 4 people you meet, thanking someone, or yielding to someone else while walking or driving ("you go first") can change your whole experience of your day. What small acts of kindness would *you* appreciate if someone else did them for *you*? Do these things for others and notice how you feel.

4. **Practice appreciating the efforts of others.** Everything that comes to us in life is the result of the kind actions of others. When we stop to notice how many ways we are helped in our lives rather than complaining about what we aren't getting, our gratitude grows.

5. **Every day, without even thinking, we may say "hello" or "thank you" or "have a good day." Change these from merely polite, automatic gestures to sincere expressions of appreciation.** How? Focus in the present moment and really *see* the person you're speaking to. Notice that this person is a miraculous being, temporarily appearing in this amazing world—just as you are!

6. **Whatever ideas you may have about kindness, be determined to be kind.** Don't let yourself be stopped by fear! Just for a moment now, think of a situation where you've noticed yourself turning away from being kind to someone. Imagine yourself turning toward that person and doing some act of kindness for them.

7. **Even a small act of kindness, such as considering others' feelings, counts.** Are you intimidated or irritated by someone at

work? Try to remember that they're a human being with feelings, too. Their irritating behavior is likely due to unresolved pain they're carrying. Within every one of us, there is hidden heartbreak. The surprise of kindness can heal the heart.

Enjoy the peace, love, and goodness of your heart. Enjoy sharing that with others!

5 Ways to Transform
Fear and Self-Doubt
into Peace and Happiness

....

WE HUMAN BEINGS HAVE an amazing capacity to form positive mental habits. Every day we have innumerable opportunities to *change the channel.* We can make the shift from a fearful state of self-doubt to an empowered state of peace and happiness.

Here are 5 great ways to cultivate the positive mental habit of peace and happiness, every day:

1. **As soon as you wake up in the morning, practice feeling grateful and surprised:** "I'm awake! I receive the gift of this day as a valuable opportunity to take positive actions with a positive view. As I keep going, I will develop an effortless, positive habit."

2. **Spend a few minutes just feeling your breathing, coming in and going out.** Appreciate that this process of breathing, which we rarely think about, is giving us life moment by moment. It doesn't even matter what we think or feel—life loves us enough to bring us fully into existence, breath by breath!

3. **Let go of any concerns about success or failure.** This doesn't mean we don't set intentions. Certainly, we make efforts to succeed. We simply recognize that fearful thoughts about success and failure just don't help. Therefore, see clearly that those thoughts are only a distraction and an energy drain. Above all, don't become fascinated by them.

4. **Replace any fearful thoughts with encouraging, creative ones.** As you develop the clarity that fearful thoughts don't help, it becomes easier and easier to dismiss them. Enjoy encouraging yourself with creative ideas instead: "I can smile and stretch right now, and look up at the sky." Creative thoughts can be a simple flip: "I doubt myself so much! What happens if I doubt my doubting?" Or imagine whimsical actions; we rarely think to do this when negative thoughts and feelings are holding us back. "I can draw a picture of my room with the furniture on the ceiling." A funny drawing can destroy the effect of a recurring negative experience: "When Uncle Joe is telling me how worthless I am, I see him in a chair that's glued to the ceiling—he's hanging upside down with everything falling out of his pockets."

5. **Recognize that there is no judge of your life—no one you have to please.** We developed certain habitual thinking patterns in our childhood and teenage years when we were being watched and judged. As a result, we might require some time to reprogram ourselves into realizing that we're not required to please anyone. Remember that focusing on pleasing others is a fearful orientation. It erodes our self-respect. Recognize that "trying to please" is merely an outdated, fearful thinking pattern. Remember that fearful thoughts never help. Then choose to cultivate a sense of mature self-respect. When we do this, we no longer speak to ourselves with guilt or self-judgment. Instead, we speak to ourselves with encouragement about accomplishing our own genuine values and interests, because we're worth it!

MEET THE CHALLENGE TO STAY KIND!

I am often amazed at how simple and beneficial these ideas are. And yet it has been difficult throughout human history for a high percentage of humanity to understand and practice them. And for whatever reason, in our technical age, it seems to have become more challenging for people to practice kindness. The constant and instantaneous flow of information presented to us on our devices in ever more sophisticated ways influences us, mesmerizes us, and keeps us in a state of stress!

Consider that it has never been easy for humanity to connect with and hold on to kindness and integrity. Therefore, you can feel proud of the effort you make. Through our resolve to cultivate kind and loving habit patterns, we are uplifting not only ourselves, but everyone. Let's explore the journey together!

How Can I Be
More Confident?

....

SOMETIMES PEOPLE SAY, "I have no confidence in myself. I don't have *low* self-esteem, I have *no* self-esteem! I always feel I'm not good enough. What should I do?"

When I hear such things in my clinical practice, I try to help people be playful. If they say they have no confidence, I might say, "Are you sure? Are you confident that you have no confidence?" If they say yes, I say, "Well then, see, you do have confidence! You just need to apply it in other areas."

"You can stop being so confident about only negative things," I tell them. "It's an option to do that if you want to, of course, but go ahead and be confident about positive things, too." And then that begins a conversation that continues to unfold in a helpful way.

When someone says "self-esteem"—and this goes for confidence too, because people often talk about these things as if they're things, as if they're substances—point out that there's no such thing as self-esteem. It's not a thing we have acquired. It's just a label for an activity we're doing.

One reason my approach is unique, at least as far as I've seen in 30 years of practicing hypnotherapy, is that I recognize that language is inherently hypnotic and also that thinking is inherently hypnotic. Because hypnosis simply means suggestion. So, every time you're listening to your internal dialogue and it tells you, "Do this, do that," and you do it—or your internal critic tells you you're a dummy and you instantly feel bad—you're accepting suggestions.

Another aspect of the hypnotic nature of language is nouns. We're taught that nouns are things, so when you use a noun, either subtly or explicitly, in a very vivid way, you're hallucinating a "thing." And there really is no thing there. All there is, really, is an activity.

So, it's not that we need to have more confidence. It's not that we lack self-esteem, as in "Oh, where can I get some self-esteem?" because self-esteem is simply a noun that masks a process we're doing. We don't see it, but we're feeding ourselves a stream of negative hypnotic suggestions: "I'm not good enough, I'm not as good as he is, I'm not as good as she is," or "I should do this, I have to do that…" And then we feel bad!

On top of that, we label that bad feeling as "no self-esteem." No. We work perfectly. Anybody who believed those negative suggestions would feel the same way. So, I often tell people who are in the midst of this kind of suffering, "Look, this is not a problem. It just shows that you work perfectly." You just need to change your activity as opposed to believing that there's something wrong with you and that you're defective. No. It's just that you're doing an activity that perfectly creates that bad feeling.

We need to understand that we're already master hypnotists. We've just been schooled in hypnosis without its being directly pointed out to us as such. We don't learn that we can generate positive suggestions because we're already habituated to believing the negative ones.

"THAT MAY BE SO AND …"— AN EXERCISE FOR BUILDING SELF-ESTEEM

Self-esteem is a label for a mental activity. If you change the activity, it can change how you feel. Think of a negative message you heard in your internal dialogue today, or generate one now. For example, the first thought says, "You're so slow-minded about math." And the second thought agrees, "Yeah, that's true."

Are you feeling bad yet? If so, that shows you work perfectly! Now, here's the fun part. Whenever you hear such a negative thought, you're going to add, "**That may be so, and…**" (then fill in the blank with a good quality, something you like about yourself or what you do).

So, the next time your mind generates a negative thought such as, "You never could carry a tune," respond with a positive thought, like this: "**That may be so, and …** you may also recall that I'm a good cook who enjoys sharing food with others. How generous!"

Try it and let me know how it goes. Good luck!

6

Facing Illness, Aging, Death, and the Holidays

Dealing with a Diagnosis of Terminal Illness

....

FOR MOST OF US, WHETHER it is we ourselves or someone we love who receives a diagnosis of terminal illness—the news stops us in our tracks. There is a gap where our mind simply halts or even shuts down. After that moment, our mind may go in many different directions. We may feel fear, grief, or shock. Or, if we have been harboring some resentment toward the person receiving this news, we may even feel a little bubble of gratification rising to the surface.

After these first few moments of unself-conscious responses, we begin to form a strategy about how to deal with the diagnosis emotionally on an ongoing basis. Many of us don't realize at this point that we can choose what emotions we will feel and how we will relate to this new, unexpected context in our life.

The idea of "choosing what emotions to feel" may sound just plain wrong. It might even strike you as an insulting and unreasonable thing to say if you hear it while first considering the finality of the diagnosis. This is especially true if in that moment you're feeling heartbroken about it. For this reason, in considering our power of choice, it is important to recognize that there is a difference between unself-conscious *feeling responses* and self-conscious *emotions*.

WHAT IS AN UNSELF-CONSCIOUS FEELING RESPONSE?

Unself-conscious feelings are organic and spontaneous. They are not created by your personality or by your morality, and they do not contain any personal bias. Calling these feelings "organic and spontaneous" simply means we all feel them, regardless of our value system or who we think we are.

Unfortunately, the moment we experience the energy of these human feelings, it is typical that we almost immediately channel that energy into the container of our personality structure ("I'm falling apart! I have to keep it together!"). This includes our sense of morality ("What's wrong with me, I should be feeling sad. Actually I feel glad—I must be a horrible person!").

Only then do our unself-conscious feelings become emotions. Emotions—and we're talking about the negative, problematic ones here—are always a response to self-conscious storylines.

SELF-CONSCIOUS EMOTIONS

Since we have the power to choose our thoughts, we also can choose what emotions to have. Why? Because choosing our thoughts means we can choose what storyline to identify with, what reference point to take. It just takes a bit of coaching to reclaim this power of choice.

Okay, so maybe you haven't received such a diagnosis, nor do you know anyone who has. In that case, consider the example of someone learning to deal with the traumatic emotions triggered by a divorce. In our society, divorce is an experience shared by a vast number of people. Learning that your partner wants a divorce triggers a strong emotional response that is very similar to the response triggered by receiving a diagnosis of terminal illness. Both kinds of news come as a sharp and penetrating signal of the end of life as we've known it.

By looking into the divorce example, we can gain important insights about relating to our mind. Looking deeply, we can discover the difference between feelings and emotions. And being able to identify the difference between feelings and emotions as they are happening provides direct assistance for dealing with a diagnosis of terminal illness.

A client once came to me in a state of agony. He was recently divorced and to his chagrin had discovered that his ex already had a lover. Since learning this, the man had been frequently waking up at night feeling as though he were suffocating. It came out that he believed he was psychically tuning into his ex and her new lover as they were engaged in passionate lovemaking. For him, the experience was not only oppressive but, because in those moments he felt that he couldn't breathe, it was also terrifying.

I asked him if he could agree that, at any given moment on earth, there are millions of couples making love, even as we sat there talking. He agreed. I pointed out that he was breathing easily. I then asked him to take the vision of his ex and her lover making love and place that picture into his mental picture of those millions of people making love throughout the world. After doing this, the man reported he had stopped waking up feeling suffocated.

What happened? By doing this simple exercise of looking at this new expanded mental picture, the man realized that his ex and her lover—and whatever they might be doing—had no special power over him. He had only been giving them power in his imagination by how he thought about the 2 of them and by means of the story he'd created about them (and about himself in relation to them).

THE POWER OF A STORYLINE

Expanding his vision with this new picture—one that included all of humanity—allowed this man to see his ex and her new lover as "just people." It was obvious to him that people are making love all the time and that thinking about all of those people had never caused him to feel suffocated!

By expanding the context and seeing the bigger story, right away my client stopped making his ex and her lover into special beings with special power over him. He could let them be "just people" making love just the way millions of other people do all over the world, all the time. This freed him from his self-imposed drama of personal agony. He had chosen a different story and a new way of seeing the situation that freed him from the self-diminishing storyline that to him had felt, quite literally, suffocating.

That wasn't the end of it, however. My client still felt deep sadness associated with separating from his ex. That was only human, a natural energetic shift. The loss of someone who has been important in our lives carries with it an equally natural experience of grief. It needs no additional storyline; it is naturally occurring, and in time that grief lessens in intensity.

Once this man stopped adding a self-diminishing storyline to his experience of losing his wife, he was able to relate to his grief in a much healthier way. He stopped punishing himself by disturbing his sleep and generating a feeling of shortness of breath, and he became able to bear his grief.

Feeling simple grief without the embellishment of any "poor me" storylines allowed him to experience his heart becoming more responsive to the suffering of other people. As he allowed the experience of the vast expanse of human suffering that includes others to replace the contracted personality suffering that excludes others, this man loosened his grip on the mask he was presenting to others … and thus became a more real human being.

Receiving a diagnosis of a terminal illness, much like hearing one's partner say they want a divorce, triggers powerful feelings as well as more personal, story-driven emotions. As we feel the physical energy of shock, we may think, "Why me? Why now? What did I do to deserve this?" These thoughts in turn can lead us to generate further storylines, such as "reasons" why us, why now, and why we might "deserve" to die. As these storylines take hold, they pave the way for a host of painful emotions—anger, resentment, and the rest—to hijack our experience and sap our strength.

Of course, regardless of a sense of deservingness, we all will die one day. The main difference with a diagnosis of terminal illness is that our death is less likely to occur suddenly. And thus, we have time to consider how we will meet it.

WAYS TO WORK WITH YOUR MIND IN DEALING WITH A TERMINAL ILLNESS

- **First, guard against narrow "poor me" storylines.** Practice generating an expanded storyline that opens you to appreciate that you're experiencing human suffering as all humans do, not a unique personal suffering. Practice thinking, "In this moment, there are millions of people who are going through situations like this and suffering just as I am suffering." Then open your heart to them— and consciously want them to feel support and comfort.

- **Then, as best you can, *relax and breathe.*** As you inhale, welcome as many suffering beings as you can visualize into your heart. And as you exhale, send out feelings of loving kindness to them. Imagine that their suffering diminishes. Consciously desire for their relief to be real, even if your logical thinking mind tries to tell you it's foolish. If this exercise makes you feel a bit better, notice that and record it in some way. Say or write or draw or sing how you feel.

- **Third, take the attitude that you can generate *blessing and healing power.*** Why not?! We all know we can generate negative power by hurting and scaring ourselves and others. If we can do that, then we can definitely do the opposite—shift our power toward blessing thoughts, kind thoughts. Choosing and practicing this attitude can make all the difference in our experience, moment to moment.

- **And last, *welcome natural grief.*** Breathe into it. As best you can, breathe into the grief with an attitude that you are willing for it to last forever. Adopting this courageous attitude can eliminate seeds of impatience, fear, and resentful thinking before they get a chance to sprout into something worse.

Life is temporary. In every case, birth is a diagnosis of terminal illness. Don't trick yourself into living in a storyline that implies you are immortal and can afford to waste time indulging in superficial negativity. A diagnosis of a terminal illness can be a wake-up call that inspires us to fully live a life of generosity and kindness while we can.

Good luck!

How to Deal
with the Fear
of Aging and Death

....

"Treat every moment as your last.
It is not preparation for something else."
— Shunryū Suzuki Roshi

AGING IS A WAKE-UP CALL.

On my 25th birthday, I felt the fear of aging for the first time. Later, crossing the midpoint of my third decade of life made me realize I would soon be 30 and then "over the hill" before I knew it.

No more being perpetually young. For a short time, I felt trapped. But then I took stock of my thinking and realized such useless fear would get me nowhere. I decided to live well while I had the chance. That seemed a lot better than focusing on my inevitable aging and death. Because that's just morbid, right?

Ironically, at that time I was studying and practicing Zen Buddhist meditation with the great teacher Shunryū Suzuki Roshi. Zen Buddhism, like all schools of Buddhism, puts a great emphasis on remembering—and directly meditating on—change and death.

One of the first teachings of the Buddha was the instruction to recognize that everything changes and that once you are born, sickness, old age, and death are inevitable. This teaching is often misunderstood in the West as morbid or nihilistic. This was the mistake I had just made!

Meditation on impermanence and death is a profoundly helpful practice when done properly, without a "poor me" mentality. Looking directly at the impermanence and fragility of life can save us from arrogance, the numbing effects of an attitude of entitlement, and from greed, all of which depend on holding onto the notion that we're immortal and that our "stuff" is permanent.

Instead of meditating on change, aging, and death, we Westerners (and many people throughout the world, for that matter) tend to distract ourselves from this reality instead. One way we do that is by entertaining beliefs about heaven. There is nothing inherently wrong with such a belief if you hold it as an operating theory—something that might be true, but the jury's still out. That means you continue to evaluate whether believing in heaven helps you improve the quality of your life. If you find such a belief doesn't serve you, it may be time to look for a better belief that does help you improve the quality of your life.

On the other hand, if you forget that "heaven" is a belief and begin treating it as an absolute truth, it's easy to get into various kinds of trouble. Treating *any* belief as an absolute truth, something we don't dare question, ends up making us closed-minded. And as we know, human beings throughout history have been deluded into hating and killing each other as a result of fighting over beliefs they decided to treat as unquestionable truths.

So, let's consider the result of becoming closed-minded about our beliefs. If doing this leads us to fear and hate and destroy one another, I would say that holding beliefs in a closed-minded way does not improve the quality of our lives. Despite the obviousness of this logic, we often resort to holding closed-minded beliefs anyway, clinging to them in an effort to escape our understandable (if unhelpful) fear of aging and death.

THE 5 MOST IMPORTANT THINGS
TO KNOW ABOUT THE FEAR OF AGING

1. **Fear is based on imagination.** All fears are imaginary. In this regard, a fear of aging is no different than any other fear. You

can't be afraid of your actual future. It hasn't happened yet! You can only be afraid of your negative fantasies about what will become of you. And you have a choice as to whether you continue to generate negative fantasies.

2. **Fearful thinking makes you squeeze and stress yourself mentally, emotionally, and physically.** If you put your effort and energy into this squeezing effort, you're setting yourself up to suffer. Why? Because squeezing and stressing yourself is degrading to your health. Stressing out also inhibits your ability to exercise good judgment and make good choices.

3. **Aging, the possibility of pain, and the inevitability of death are facts of life, yes. But they do *not require* us to practice creating fearful fantasies.** We can imagine staying healthy and aging gracefully. Such positive mental exercises not only create a more pleasant environment in our mind but also help keep us healthy. So, why not switch to uplifting fantasies!

4. **Fearful thinking is a waste of time!** Fear comes along when we've made up our mind that something negative is bound to happen. To do this, first we have to create a false certainty. How many times have you worried about something that ended up not happening? Maybe you found yourself shaking your head as you realized what a waste of time and energy that was!

5. **Fearful thinking is a *present-time activity* just like all activities.** We forget this when we get involved with fearful thoughts. We go into a trance of living in the past or a future fantasy, losing all awareness that we're simply alive right here, right now. All of our freedom and power are available now and only now—we can relax and open up, or we can squeeze

and contract. Does it make sense to exercise the free use of your power to get upset about a negative past that's over or a fantasy future that may never come? Doing that, don't we miss the present opportunity to enjoy the gift of life right now?

Fearful thinking—whatever we're fearful of—distracts us from developing a sense of wonder and gratitude for this amazing life we have. Every moment is new. Each moment is an entirely new opportunity to experience life just as it is, right on the spot!

Someday our lives will end, it's true. So, why ruin life while we're in the midst of living it? Instead of dulling our mind and senses with fear, let's enliven ourselves and brighten our mind and senses.

To do this, we only have to pause with wonder and gratitude for the gift of life—not the gift of "Jack's life" or "Alicia's life," but life itself. Our idea of who we are may be filled with unpleasant judgments and memories, but we can feel free to skip all that and turn toward life's innate wondrousness.

Focus on the wonder of life as it manifests as each being and everything in each fresh moment. Focus on the fact that you couldn't even complain or think fearful thoughts if life were not giving you the gift of your conscious, living intelligence, moment by moment... brand-new in every brand-new moment!

How Bad
Holiday Memories
Can Actually Help You

....

IT'S NO SECRET THAT our personal associations with the holidays can bring us sorrow as well as joy. Extremes of happiness and sadness may have good cause. In my case, wonderful memories of warm celebrations filled with great food, gifts, and rowdy cousins to play with are tempered by the memory of my 20th year when, after enduring a 6-month struggle with cancer, my mother died shortly after Christmas.

When we experience the commingling of powerful positive and negative experiences, we're presented with an opportunity to challenge deep tendencies of our mind. Like me, even as you're appreciating the aroma of a turkey dinner being prepared, the memories it calls up may also cause a pang in your heart. But instead of diving into feeling small and falling into a dark mood, in that moment we can actively choose to connect with appreciation and joy instead.

I'm not recommending avoiding or repressing our natural grief, or stuffing bad holiday memories or old hurt feelings. What I am recommending is how we can choose our experience in each moment. We can decide to experience the richness of whatever that moment contains, rather than feeling victimized by the memories it calls up.

TRY THIS TO CONNECT WITH GRATITUDE AND JOY

1. **Release any notion that it is "selfish" or "bad" to invite abundance and joy into your life**. The only thing that can make it "bad" would be if you asked for good things at the expense of others. Again and again, invite abundance, joy, compassion, and wisdom for yourself and for everyone. Then relax and open to it.

2. **Release the images and stories about yourself that tend to convince you that you are small**, hopeless, helpless, unlovable, or unimportant. Such ideas are trances of personality and they cause us to suffer. This kind of painful thinking torments us because it goes largely unexamined.

3. **Challenge the self-critical stories.** Practice asking, "In order to have this problem, who do I have to believe I am?" or "What do I have to believe is true about me?" Then challenge the "truth" of the answer you come up with.

4. **Practice contemplating the greatness and mystery of life.** Go outside and look at the sky. Take a moment to remember the myriad lives that are sustained by this planet. Consider the many nourishing breaths you take in any given day. You yourself are a full manifestation of this same greatness and mystery.

5. **Recognize that you are greater than what you think about yourself.** A great saint once said about the practice of contemplating the true nature of oneself versus the false notions of oneself: "One who meticulously measures the length of his shadow, before trying to leap over it, cannot be said to understand anything about a shadow. Similarly, the one who, after arduous study of the scriptures, comes to some definitive

conclusion about the Self, has failed to understand it. Words recoil from the Self, so how can the intellect, which functions entirely by means of words, understand anything about it?"

6. **Trust yourself.** Practice this again and again: Simply rest in the present moment, center your awareness in your heart, and ignore any thinking that judges your effort or distracts you from this effort to rest in simple, open awareness.

7. **Recognize that prayer and worry share the same basic template.** They are both focused, emotion-laden thought about a given subject. Therefore, see that worry is just negative prayer. We tend to get what we pray for. So, when you find yourself worrying, instead of fighting it, take the subject of concern out of worry mode … and instead, pray as joyfully and confidently as possible for the blessing that would fulfill the concern and bring about the greatest good for all. It's a most important, empowering practice!

May these simple practices support you in having a wonderful holiday season … and may they stay with you for the rest of your life!

And while we're on the subject, you may enjoy checking out our popular webinar called *Family Matters: 5 Ways to Stop Your Past from Screwing Up Your Future.* This audio program includes guided visualizations, slideshow presentations, and class discussions. It's available now in the Finding True Magic online shop at shop.findingtruemagic.com.

Getting Clear
about Fear

....

I WAS ASKED RECENTLY, "Given how much violence has increased in our society, isn't it healthy to fear for my child's safety?" The welfare of our children is a compelling natural concern for almost all living beings—not just humans. That concern is built into the parental instinct of whales, dolphins, elephants, and many other animals.

At this writing, in America we are experiencing a degree of potential danger in public places that most of us did not previously think was possible. We're living in a new world where schools, churches, and shopping centers can no longer be assumed to be safe gathering places for ourselves or our children.

Many people in our society, especially those with light skin, have long taken for granted a certain level of safety. Frankly, if we're white, the existing dangers have remained invisible to us or been relegated by our minds to other remote parts of the world. But if we're people of color, we may never have felt secure even in our own country and now we likely feel much less safe.

But now, whatever level of safety we once expected or hoped for is being destroyed by increasing incidents of domestic terrorism in our country. The violent images we've seen reported in the news and online raise an especially vivid area of concern for us: the well-being of our children. And what may begin as a reasonable concern can sometimes grow into persistent worry, anxiety, and fear.

On this issue of fearing for one's children, I am not merely an armchair philosopher. Long ago, I lost my firstborn child after a long terminal illness, one which year after year made it increasingly difficult for her to breathe. So, I know what it is like to fear losing your child, and I know what it is like to lose her.

THE DIFFERENCE BETWEEN HEALTHY FEAR AND OBSESSION
In my clinical work with people, I've discovered there is a lot of confusion around fear. People often believe they "have to" be afraid of terrible possibilities. They think this fear and worry are proof of their love and care.

But if I say, "I worry because I care, and I'm afraid because I care," what else am I saying? Actually, I'm suggesting it is somehow good or virtuous for me to stay fearful and to worry. But does my thinking this way really equal caring?

The fact is, fearful thinking and worry are never helpful. And when we keep ourselves engaged in constant worry and fear about our children's safety, our fear can even become harmful. Why? Because obsessive worry blocks us from having the mental clarity to create effective solutions, even those regarding our children's safety.

First, we have to get clear that when we talk about "unhealthy fear" or "fearful obsession," we're not talking about the well-known fight-flight-freeze response. This is a very helpful, built-in protective response born of our natural instinct and need for survival. We don't need to try to eliminate that.

The fear that causes us problems is *psychological* fear: the fearful thinking and storytelling that keeps our body sparking adrenaline and other stress-related hormones that degrade our mental and physical well-being. This destructive mental activity blocks the beneficial mental activity of constructive, solution-oriented brainstorming, which is what we need to meet our challenges.

What does all this mean? Your worry and stress do not help your child! In fact, your worry and stress teach your child to be worried and stressed. Children look to Mom, Dad, their teachers, and caregivers to learn how to respond to whatever life presents.

4 STEPS YOU CAN TAKE TO SUPPORT YOUR CHILD'S SAFETY

1. **Learn about child development.** Most importantly, understand that children are NOT little adults. Before the age of 7, generally, a child cannot discriminate or evaluate. They don't know that you as an adult have an inner, often conflicted life that triggers your emotional reactions. If you tell them it's "their fault" and that they are "bad" (child's translation: "forever unlovable"), they will believe you! By working with your reactions and weighing the words you say to your child, you can protect them from self-loathing, which is often more damaging than any physical harm they may survive.

2. **Using age-appropriate language, let children know that adults have inner lives.** You can explain to them that adults get confused in ways that trigger them to act angry and sad. Make it clear to your child that your emotional state is not their fault or their responsibility. Let them see your vulnerable humanity. This shows children the inner strength you have to treat yourself with kindness and respect in the midst of your emotional struggle, and it shows you taking responsibility for your own feelings. Sharing this way enables your child to understand that they are not the cause of others' emotional suffering. And it gives them a healthy model for dealing with their *own* emotional life—with self-kindness, self-respect, and courage.

3. **Relate to your child with kindness, respect, and encouragement.** This is not a moral guideline. It is a practical, strategic guideline. Let your child know they are loved, valued, and worthy of basic respect no matter what mistakes they make (even destructive ones) and no matter what circumstances

they find themselves in. In other words, do not shame your child or put them down.

4. **Give your child the support to honor and express their true thoughts, desires, and values without fear of being punished or ridiculed for sharing them.** The sad fact is that even in these times of escalating physical violence, the source of the greatest harm to our children is that our society all too commonly operates from a misguided sense of entitlement to mistreat children, shame them, or take them for granted. Yes, we may be their parents or guardians, but we do not own them!

WHAT ELSE CAN WE DO TO HELP OUR CHILDREN?

In 32 years of working with clients in private practice, I have learned that the core of a great many problems is often some form of learned self-rejection, a numbness to one's own true needs and desires, and even sometimes a learned self-hatred. These ways of thinking are delusions. So why are they passed on generation after generation? Because in large part, we rarely recognize the delusions we learned when we were gullible children.

Recently someone told me that her father was "never abusive and was always kind." A few minutes later, she mentioned that her father frequently said he "didn't like whiners." My heart sank, hearing this lack of empathy. The person sharing this story clearly agreed with that harsh viewpoint.

I wasn't entirely surprised, though. A child will often adopt an insult like this as their own point of view. This is a survival mechanism: "If I agree with them, they won't hurt me." When a parent criticizes a young child this way, the child doesn't understand that the criticism is directed at an unacceptable behavior (whining) and not at them as a person. Nevertheless, the child feels the comment as a painful, visceral rejection of their entire being. And in the worst cases, the parent actually means it that way.

Children who take on and internalize such negative self-messages may suffer for years in flimsy relationships or experience long periods of self-imposed isolation and loneliness. This is the kind of long-term harm that we can and should be genuinely concerned about. We can do everything in our power to avoid passing on this damaging criticism, worry, and fear to our children by putting focus and energy into kind, encouraging, creative thinking.

Of course, we must do all we can to bring safety to our communities, streets, and neighborhoods so that our children are free to enjoy and explore growing up. But even as we work to protect our children's safety, we can place our focus and our energy where it can do the greatest good day-to-day. Let's give ourselves to the worthy project of kindly healing our own confusions, delusions, and wounds so that we don't pass on these harmful toxins to our children.

We may not be able to shield our child from every harm, but we do have the power to change our careless words into caring ones, to transform our fear into fierce love, and trade our worry for wisdom. May you and your loved ones be safe. May kindness flourish in our communities.

How to Keep Your Courage in the Age of the Pandemic, Terrorism, and Climate Change

....

As THE TRIPLE THREATS of the pandemic, terrorism, and climate change begin to appear more immediate and personal to us, we tend to feel more afraid. Those of us accustomed to living a relatively privileged life may feel ashamed that we're afraid. This unfortunate combination of feelings makes it difficult to develop a good course of action.

We can feel ashamed of our fear because we know that every day, throughout the world, thousands of people are experiencing horrific suffering—suffering that we very much want to avoid. That's understandable, to be sure. But to go deeper into worry, shame, or guilt makes our inner state worse, not better. So clearly, it's not an effective strategy.

It's best to use the awareness of the suffering of others to connect with our gratitude and courage. We often forget, as we engage in the speedy activities of daily life, that we belong to a larger world. Along with everyone else, we are mortal.

We're completely invested in our many plans for the future, but actually death can come at any moment. Far from being merely morbid, this sobering thought will keep us sane by helping us maintain our courage in the age of pandemics, terrorism, and climate change. Ironically, when we welcome the awareness of our mortality, it causes us to feel more genuine joy in our lives. Just try it.

Rather than feeling guilty or ashamed of feeling fear about contracting a deadly virus, or being victimized by threats of terrorism or climate catastrophes, we can shift our focus when we feel a sense of dread. We can make it an opportunity to feel grateful for whatever good we have in our lives. We can keep our hearts open with courage and dignity. We can choose this focus again and again.

We're all going to die one day in any case, so there's no need to drive ourselves crazy about it in the meantime.

In my experience, the best way to overcome fear is to recognize that fearful thinking is never your friend. Fearful fantasies will never help you make the right choices for your life.

With a clear head, you can decide how best to contribute in a positive way toward a better world. And you'll find that you make the best decisions and have the greatest mental clarity when you're vividly experiencing a sense of gratitude. At such times, you're not being ruled by fear. And when you're not ruled by fear, then even when fear is present in your mind and emotions, your actions are naturally courageous.

If you would like a little extra help to work with fearful thinking, you could check out one of my most popular hypnosis audios: *Stress Relief, Rejuvenation, and Empowerment.* Or this other one: *Becoming Fearless and Compassionate.* Both have been helpful to a great many people and are available in the Finding True Magic store at shop.findingtruemagic.com.

About the Authors

....

Jack Elias, CHT has studied and practiced Buddhism since 1967, first with Zen teacher Suzuki Roshi, then with Buddhist teachers Chögyam Trungpa Rinpoche and Dzogchen Ponlop Rinpoche. A hypnotherapist and NLP trainer since 1988, Jack is known for his smart, boisterous humor and for distilling profound insights into simple techniques anyone can practice with lasting positive results.

Ceci Miller, MFA is a longtime meditator and a student of Buddhism with Dzogchen Ponlop Rinpoche since 2005. An author, communications consultant, and trainer, Ceci is a certified instructor of the Emotional Rescue Method. She has written, edited, and consulted on a wide variety of social and emotional learning (SEL) publications for both adults and children.